THE MAGIC OF HONEY

The ancients appreciated the glorious taste of honey. Health food enthusiasts have discovered, once again, honey's powers—its delicious flavors, medicinal qualities and natural nutritional values.

Here is everything you'd like to know about honey— its role in history, its wondrous energy and health-giving attributes, its legendary possibilities as a fertility food and aphrodisiac.

Here too are honey recipes for cooking and baking with honey, making jams, jellies and preserves, honey syrups for canning and freezing fruits, honey in drinks, and much, much more.

THE MAGIC OF HONEY

DOROTHY PERLMAN

 AVON
PUBLISHERS OF BARD, CAMELOT, DISCUS, EQUINOX AND FLARE BOOKS

4

AVON BOOKS
A division of
The Hearst Corporation
959 Eighth Avenue
New York, New York 10019

Copyright © 1971 by Nash Publishing.
Published by arrangement with Nash Publishing.
Library of Congress Catalog Card Number: 73-167506.

ISBN: 0-380-00029-6

First Avon Printing, June, 1974.

AVON TRADEMARK REG. U.S. PAT. OFF. AND
FOREIGN COUNTRIES, REGISTERED TRADEMARK—
MARCA REGISTRADA, HECHO EN CHICAGO, U.S.A.

Printed in the U.S.A.

The Magic of Honey

CONTENTS

PART I HONEY: ITS HISTORY AND MAGIC

1. What Is Honey? 9 to 15...
2. Honey: The Health Food 17 to 28...
3. Honey: How It Is Made 29 to 35.....
4. Composition of Honey 37 to 44...
5. Characteristics of Honey 45 to 50...
6. Variations and Classifications 51 to 61...
7. Honey in History 63 to 72
8. Honey in Religion 73
9. Honey as a Healer 81
10. Honey in Symbolism, Poetry and Proverbs 91
11. Uses of Honey 97

PART II COOKING WITH HONEY

1. Magical, Mystical Cookery with Honey 103
2. Helpful Hints for Cooking and Baking 105
3. Jellies, Jams and Preserves Made with Honey 109
4. Honey Syrups for Canning and Freezing
   Fruits 111
5. Honey in Drinks 113
6. Other Honey Drinks 119
7. Breads, Cakes, Cookies, Muffins 123
8. Honey Pies and Desserts 131
9. Meats, Fowls, Vegetables 137
10. Honey Happenings 143
11. Honey and Ecology 153

Part I

HONEY: ITS HISTORY AND MAGIC

8/

1

WHAT IS HONEY?

Honey is a natural food manufactured by honeybees from the nectar and pollen of flowers in a natural atmosphere of beauty and love known to no other workers in the world. Its form, its texture, its color, reflect nature at her most voluptuous.

Originally created by bees as food for bees, it has been usurped, abetted and enjoyed by man from ancient times to the present. And, from all indications, it will be enjoyed even more in the future—if the bees, flowers and voluptuous nature stay with us.

Honey is a *healthy* food because it contains natural sugar, ready to be used by the body. It doesn't require a complex digestive process like cane and beet sugars.

Though there may be those who don't like honey, there's no record of anyone being allergic to honey or being harmed by it. Throughout the ages people have lived better, loved better, because of honey. Stories of its powers are legion—some legend, some true. Upon beggar and king alike it bestows its bounty.

Honey! Its very sound evokes pictures of tenderness, pleasure, harmony, simplicity, love. Is it any wonder young people today in search of a simple, wholesome life are eating honey—by the spoonfuls, in chunks, in tea, on homemade bread—in dozens of ways.

Honey as a food mingles well with a wide assortment of other health foods: whole grain flours and cereals, soybeans, natural unpolished brown rice, sprouts, wheat germ, sunflower seeds, pumpkin seeds, sesame seeds, chia seeds—to name just a few.

Honey and milk are practically soul mates. All through history, as far back as biblical times, milk and honey have shared joint billing. The phrase, "flowing with milk and honey," connoted health, wealth, plenty. Palestine notably was called the land of milk and honey. Poetry, literature, music abound with references to honey—always in a pleasant sense. (Except, of course, when someone says it's sticky, which it is. But it doesn't stick to the teeth like other sugars.)

Honey took on other connotations in history and folklore—connotations of fertility and sexuality. How it all happened no one knows, just as no one can state for sure when and where honey was first used by men. In the simple world of long ago when they lived close to the soil, people learned from nature. Associating honey with sex and fertility was natural. Beehives dripping honey became a symbol of loins dripping desire.

People have always sought aphrodisiacs, for substances that would enhance their own, or their partner's sexual powers. Honey built up a reputation among peasants and royalty alike for being a love food. And it's maintained that reputation among many people to this day.

Some of what we know about honey comes from speculation and conjecture, but more comes from practical experiences with honey—people experiences, so to speak.

This is particularly true when it comes to what is known as "folk medicine." Honey has been used for cuts, bruises, chapped skin, constipation, diarrhea, sore throat, even warts. And it seems to have helped to alleviate these conditions.

Honey has been used as a facial pack in beauty parlors and at home, in hand lotions, in curing pipe bowls, in chewing gum, as a spray adherent, as a center for golf balls, as an antifreeze mixture for auto radiators, and as a preservative for eggs in cold storage.

Today honey is employed as a vehicle for such medicines as cough syrups and salves. Doctors recommend it for feeding infants, especially those suffering from rickets, scurvy, malnutrition, anemia, inflammation of the intestine, and the effects of prematurity. The latter usage is particularly noteworthy in those parts of the world where doctors and people rely on natural methods to cure ailments. Honey together with certain pollens has been successfully used in alleviating hay fever symptoms.

Whenever and wherever it is used, honey seems to impart to the user some magical essence that no one yet has been able to define or duplicate.

Honey is international. The listings in the "World's Honey Market" in the *American Bee Journal* resemble a roster of the United Nations. From

Canada to Zululand! Each country seems to take
pride in the honey it produces. Honey connoisseurs
exist in every land. They've been compared to
wine and cheese connoisseurs.

Honey appears in many ethnic foods. Yogis
(those who practice yoga) consider honey an inte-
gral part of their diet. The Hindus, among others,
believed honey had aphrodisiacal qualities. Partaking of honey constituted part of the marriage ceremony.

In early societies honey was regarded as a sacred
substance and used in making sacrifices to the
gods. Men believed their gods needed honey as
much as they themselves did. Tombs of Egyptian
kings were not considered complete without lotus
blossoms, boxes of honey cakes and jars of honey.
Honey was regarded as a symbol of eternal bliss. It
has been reported that during the excavation of
the tomb of Queen Tiy's parents in Egypt a jar of
honey was found, still in a fairly liquid state. As far
as could be determined the jar had been hermeti-
cally sealed and placed in the tomb some 3300
years before its discovery!

In ancient Egypt the bridegroom had to promise
to supply his bride with a certain amount of honey
during every year of their marriage. At the culmi-
nation of a wedding ceremony the groom said
something like this: "I take you for my wife. I
promise to furnish you annually with thirty-two
pounds of honey." (Love, cherish, and give her
honey!)

In early Hindu wedding celebrations honey was
served to the guests and the bridal pair. As part of
the ceremony the bridegroom would say: "This is
honey, the speech of my tongue is honey, and the
honey of the bee is dwelling in my mouth." It was

the custom to anoint the bride's forehead, lips, eyelids, and ear lobes with honey.

(Use of honey during wedding ceremonies was based on the belief that the purity of honey would ward off evil spirits during the celebration and insure a long, happy and fruitful marriage.)

Many Asiatic peoples believed honey to be a magical substance. They believed it affected fertility of women and livestock. The same belief prevailed with regard to their crops. By using honey in religious rites they hoped to prevent blight and pestilence from destroying their food.

The Moors are said to have regarded honey as a love stimulant. No bridegroom retired to the bridal chamber without first imbibing quantities of honey. Honey and honey wines were standard fare at wedding feasts and freely enjoyed by guests and the nuptial couple.

The concept of honey as a *love food* spilled over into Europe, where it became an important ingredient in love elixirs.

The esthetically inclined Greeks maintained a less earthy view of love and erotica. Platonic or intellectual relationships between the sexes became fashionable. Honey as an aphrodisiac was frowned upon. It became, instead, an elixir of youth. Officially and among the ruling classes this was the prevailing attitude toward sex and honey, but chances are the idea of platonic relationships didn't make much headway among the commonfolk.

The ancient Romans apparently didn't go along with the Greek concept of Platonic love, and honey made a comeback as a love food. Beekeeping was a major industry in ancient Rome. Each honey harvest heralded wild celebrations which, in turn, called for much imbibing of honey brews and much sexual activity. Some historians refer to them as "barbaric sex orgies." But then, historians, often writing long after the "happening," tend to apply their own conceptions of what is moral and right to such ancient folk customs as copulating in the fields.

Accounts of longevity among honey-drinking ancients appear often enough to cause considerable speculation about this attribute of honey.

Pliny the Elder lived in Rome between A.D. 23 and A.D. 79. He wrote extensively on the nutritional and medicinal values of honey. He believed the daily use of honey insured long life and good health. It didn't work for him even though he ate lots of honey—but not because of the honey. He met an untimely end in an attempt to rescue friends caught near the path of overflowing Vesuvian lava which destroyed the city of Pompeii.

The Essenes, an ancient Hebrew sect, were beekeepers famous for their honey and also for great age. Many were said to have lived over a hundred years.

In ancient Britain, beekeeping was a major industry and honey the principal commodity as well as an important part of the diet of every Britisher from the king to his lowliest subject. At the dawn of the Christian era Britain was said to be a paradise of honey bees. Inhabitants of the British Isles gained a reputation for longevity. But considering that they ate milk, honey, vegetables, and fruit, grown naturally in clean air, without sprays and pesticides, longevity may have resulted from a combination of honey with other natural foods rather than from honey alone. (Besides, since in ancient time plagues and pestilence were not uncommon, anyone who survived them would have had an unusually strong constitution.)

Nonetheless daily use of honey is one of those

things that usually appears in stories telling of someone's great age. Even modern beekeepers claim they live long because they raise bees and eat plenty of honey.

All in all, honey has enjoyed a lively reputation down through history. It is the oldest sweetener known to man, just about the only one until sugar cane was discovered in the New World and processed to obtain sugar, somewhere in the middle of the eighteenth century.

It must also be borne in mind that in ancient and not so ancient times the world abounded in meadowland filled with wild flowers. Bees did not have far to go for food. Woods and hillsides gave the bees homesites. Wild honeybees thrived in plentiful natural surroundings. People didn't bother to domesticate bees to the extent they do today.

Honey was considered an *ordinary* food in the kitchen, used for everyday baking and cooking; with bread, muffins, shortbreads; as sweets. Fruits were preserved in honey solutions, hams originally cured in honey.

With some exceptions, in today's modern kitchens honey is considered a *special* food. Many nutritionists believe it should be restored to its role as an everyday food, together with other natural foods.

Honey has withstood the test of time and usage, from the moment primitive man first curled his tongue around a drop of honey "falling from the sky" to the present. And, as has been written: Whoever tastes a bit of honey, tastes a bit of *magic!*

— chpt 2 —
goes fm pg 17 to pg 28...

2

HONEY: THE HEALTH FOOD

Honey is a health food because of its health-giving attributes and its unique natural source—which may account for the attributes. Man, with all his technical prowess, could never obtain from nature what the bees provide for him. Even if he had the equipment and time to collect nectar and pollen from millions of flowers he still doesn't know and can't duplicate the bees' "process" for turning nectar and pollen into honey. This process still remains one of the mysteries of nature.

Bees obtain ingredients for their product from the very womb of nature: her reproductive system. And in so doing they also participate in the process of reproduction. You might call them nature's little matchmakers.

Most flowering plants have both male and female cells and are self-pollinating. In the same plant pollen (the male sperm) falls or is blown onto the ovules (the female cells), and fertilization takes place. But plants resulting from this self-pollinization tend to be weaker than the parent plant. Generations of self-pollinated plants result in poor, scraggly progeny. (This might be compared to inbreeding among humans.)

To strengthen future generations of plants, nature provides cross-pollinization through the media of bees, birds, insects, and wind. But the bees account for most of the cross-pollinization because of their number, their industrious nature, and their food needs.

In nature's marvelous scheme of propagation she imbues the nectar with tantalizing aromas to lure the bees. (Bees have been known to travel up to fifty miles because of an alluring nectar.) As the bee extracts nectar from the flower, she brushes against the pollen, which adheres to her. Traveling from flower to flower (and she visits thousands of them in a day), she carries pollen from one to another. Bees usually work with one species of flower at a time. It's easier that way. Once they figure out how to get to the source of the nectar in a certain kind of flower they return to the same one. The second time they extract the nectar it's easier and quicker for them—and it becomes easier and quicker with repeated visits.

While searching for food for themselves so they can produce healthy progeny, honeybees promote reproduction in plants so *they*, too, can produce healthy progeny. (Maybe that's why so many people all through history claim honey is a love food and stimulates sexual appetites!)

In some respects the food requirements of a healthy bee resemble those of a healthy man. Both require protein and sugar. The bee, however, requires far less protein and far more sugar. Pollen contains a small amount of protein, and nectar contains large amounts of sugar. Not much of the protein shows up in the honey man eats, because it's often strained or filtered out to make a clear honey.

Honeybees produce food to fit their needs, which means food containing high-energy qualities. Bees during their working hours expend tremendous amounts of energy. One foraging bee visits approximately a thousand to fifteen hundred tiny florets of clover just to fill her honey-stomach—and her stomach is the size of a *pin-head!* She makes about ten thousand flights to bring a pound of nectar to the hive. On each of these flights she carries half her weight in nectar. (This could be compared to a 150-pound man with a 75-pound pack on his back running back and forth all day.)

In man's diet, honey is considered one of nature's finest energy-giving foods and one of her most remarkable. Centuries ago Greek athletes stuffed themselves with honey during their training period for the Olympic games. Swiss mountain climbers have always consumed quantities of honey for weeks prior to undertaking a dangerous climb. Long-distance swimmers and deep-sea divers do the same.

Many stories are told about the use of honey by men and women engaged in strenuous, arduous activity. One concerns the crew that volunteered to dive to the wreck of the *Lusitania*, which was sunk in the Atlantic Ocean during World War I. The men went into special training. In addition to a diet high in nutritive value they ate honey daily, increasing the amounts until, three weeks before they started their task, they were consuming a pound and a half of comb honey for breakfast every morning. And each time they came up from the sea they were given nothing to eat but a half a glass of strained honey, lemon juice, and rain water.

Another story is of the RAF pilots during World War II. In the early days of the Battle of Britain when they were practically on round-the-clock missions, pilots were fed huge quantities of honey in addition to their regular food. Upon returning from each mission they were given honey and water to help them recover from fatigue.

Also, during World War II, in the underground bomb shelters people were given rations of honey and wheat germ. It was believed this would give them a fairly balanced diet should they be forced to remain for long periods of time.

The scientists' explanation for the usefulness of large quantities of honey in strenuous and fatigue-producing activities may be summed up in the following: Simple sugars (levulose and dextrose) contained in honey help build up reserves of glycogen and blood sugar which are important in preparation for any feat of endurance.

In everyday ordinary activity man consumes energy and he requires a certain amount of reserve energy. Naturally, he doesn't need the reserves required for strenuous activity and certainly not the amount of energy a bee requires in her everyday life. But man consumes energy in other ways besides physical activity. He consumes it with tensions, anxieties, worries, which modern living supplies him in abundance.

The bee provides man with a healthy energy food claimed to be second to none: *honey.* And, it's completely natural! No one yet has "invented" honey.

In her book, *Introduction to Health Foods,* (Nash Publishing, 1971) Marjorie Miller says:

Of the eight thousand products on the shelves of our supermarkets, over five thousand have been 'invented' by biochemists since World War II.

Not so honey. Synthetic sweeteners, yes—but no synthetic honey. It may be strained, filtered, whipped, but it remains honey, without additives, preservatives, or chemicals. And the recipe hasn't changed. The bees make it the same way, with the same ingredients they used five thousand years ago. It was a natural, healthy food then. It still is.

But as healthy as honey is, not even the most ardent of its users advocates a honey-only diet. In the first place, if anyone did go on such a diet he'd probably reach a honey-saturation point and develop an intense dislike for it. Secondly, honey is not the *complete* food. It's a *natural sugar source*. It contains the carbohydrates which play an essential part in a well-balanced diet. (Sugars are carbohydrates.)

According to nutritionists a balanced diet should contain proteins, carbohydrates and fats in certain proportions. The proportions vary according to the age of the individual. Infants and growing children require more protein and carbohydrates than adults because their bodies are building tissue and muscle; also, they consume more energy.

HONEY AND REFINED SUGARS

First, to minimize any possible confusion that may arise in the reader's mind regarding the term "sugar" used in our discussion, here's the difference between the honey and the cane or beet sugars.

The sugars in honey are not the same sugars sold in bags and cartons. These latter, the bagged sugars, are refined sugars derived from sugar cane or sugar beets; they are manufactured from plant juices through an artificial processing method invented by man.

The sugars contained in honey derive from the nectar gathered by honey bees and are arrived at through a natural process unique to the bees and still unfathomed by man.

Both honey sugar and refined cane (or beet) sugar are classified as carbohydrates.

Researchers at the University of California Agricultural Experiment Station, in a recent publication, *A Handbook on Beekeeping* (J. E. Eckert, 1960), stated:

> Honey deserves a preferred place among sweets because the sugars, being in invert form, are readily assimilated. The presence of minerals, although in minute quantities, adds further to its desirability as a food. Honey also has a flavor and sweetness that tend to satisfy a craving for sweets without the use of large quantities of sugar. Its slightly laxative effect, when used to modify cow's milk in infant feeding, is considered a valuable point.

(The term *invert* may be explained simply by saying that inverted sugar found in honey has already been pre-digested by the bees. It doesn't have to go through the same digestive processes in the human stomach required by other sugars. *Inverted sugar* is more readily assimilated into the system.)

Another important difference between honey and refined sugars is: Honey is not habit-forming, while in some cases refined sugars are. A person may like the taste of honey and eat it, but he doesn't develop a craving for it. It's not addictive, whereas refined sugars have sometimes been found to be addictive.

The fact that refined sugar is artificially created is not the primary objection to its use, nor is the fact that it doesn't provide nourishment. The primary objection to its use is that it becomes a powerful stimulant in the human stomach producing an almost explosive effect upon the digestive system.

Refined sugars may be compared to combustible fuels that ignite explosively, burn at intense heat, and die out quickly. A sense of exhilaration is followed by a "let-down"; the sugar eater then feels a hunger for more sugar. That's why some people eat one piece of candy after another until they consume a whole box of candy. Often they don't really want to eat the candy, but there's a chemical effect on the digestive tract that creates a compulsive desire for more. Poorly nourished persons, children and adults alike, are highly susceptible to sugar addiction.

Healthy, well-nourished adults are better able to stand the strains to the digestive system imposed by daily use of refined sugars. But in some cases a person's system doesn't easily withstand the strain, and excessive sugar intake leads to exhaustion of the flow of weak (or latently weak) pancreatic juices, resulting in serious physical disorders.

The daily use of honey involves no such problems, because honey consists of natural sugars required by the body, easily assimilated by the system without straining the digestive tract. It is absorbed immediately and the energy it provides is stored by the body to be consumed as needed. Honey, even when it's fermented to make wine, is not considered by many a stimulant. It gives the user a pleasant feeling, a feeling of well-being—a healthy feeling. Almost without exception everyone the author interviewed about honey said it made them feel *good*.

There exist honey "fanatics" who would banish the use of refined sugars and demand that only honey be used in all areas of food production where artificially refined sugars are employed. But experts say this point of view is hardly feasible and not even desirable. First of all, they say, if everyone in the world were suddenly to eat honey to the exclusion of any and all other sweeteners there wouldn't be enough honey produced in the world to fill the demand. Also, they say that in many operations, like canning and distilling, to name only two, the use of refined sugars is preferable. Even in the home kitchen, in some instances, the use of refined sugar is more practical, particularly in making preserves, in baking and cooking. Refined sugars, when they are cooked in combination with other ingredients, place less of a strain on the digestive system than they do when eaten "as is."

The course recommended for those who are "addicted" to refined sugars is to taper off. First, the user should examine his or her diet to determine whether or not it is a balanced nutritive diet—one that includes plenty of fresh fruits and vegetables and whole grain cereals.

It is also suggested that the consumption of artificial sugar be reduced gradually, so the bodily functions will adjust. Substitute honey wherever possible, little by little. If a person is a real sugar addict he may miss the stimulation provided by sugar and find it difficult at first to substitute honey. It may take a little time, but the advantages to the digestive system are well worth the effort.

Another point to remember is that many foods besides refined sugars and honey provide necessary natural carbohydrate sources. Fresh fruit, fruit juices, fresh vegetables, vegetable juices; corn, peas, lima beans, potatoes; whole-grain breads, cereals, provide carbohydrates. A person addicted to sugar should increase his consumption of these foods, particularly the fresh fruits and vegetables.

Here are some guidelines for using sweets:

1. Use honey in coffee (if sweetening is desired), for sweet sauces used on puddings and desserts, and for syrups. Also for cake frostings and for candy. Try to avoid refined sugars in concentrated form. (Some people even eat sugar lumps.)

2. If you use refined sugars it's best to use them in diluted form—in cooked foods such as puddings, pound cake, cookies, pies. Even here, try to substitute honey partially. (This is more fully explained in the section on "Cooking with Honey.")

3. When you're tired and need a lift, drink natural fruit juices, which provide natural sugars, minerals, and vitamins, *plus* the alkaline elements essential to combat fatigue. Take a spoonful of honey, eat a sweet made with honey, or drink warm milk with a teaspoonful of honey in it.

4. If you think you're coming down with a cold it's probably advisable to discontinue all artificial sugars and syrups. Use honey and fruit juices instead.

A question many people ask is: If honey is so good and so healthy and people used it so much in olden times, why the change-over to using refined sugars?

The answer seems to be that the change was very gradual, as it is with many changes in food tastes. No one can say with certainty just when it was that people began using refined sugars instead of honey.

Up to the eighteenth century very little refined sugar was used in Europe. It was very expensive, was considered a luxury, and was used only by royalty and the wealthy. And, as often happens, the foods and fashions of the upper classes were coveted by the lower classes. Sugar became sort of a status symbol (just like eating white bread made from refined flour).

In America, too, only the upper classes could afford to buy white sugar. Farmers and poor people continued to use honey. Refined white sugar in America, too, had an aura of elegance. Anyone who could afford to eat it was considered "high class." (Americans tended to copy the Europeans in fashions of eating and clothes.)

Early in the nineteenth century Franz Achard, a German scientist, developed a process for manufacturing sugar from beets, and soon Europeans began using beet sugar. Honey ceased to be a staple in their diets. Sugar was easier to store, easier to use. Commercially, it was easier to ship. Americans followed the pattern of the Europeans and gradually sugar supplanted honey. Honey became a "special" food, a treat, instead of a staple.

The industrial era that came into full being in the middle of the nineteenth century brought about many changes influencing the switchover to sugar. Farmers migrated to cities, both in Europe and America, to work in factories. A whole new pattern of life emerged, cities developed, eating habits changed.

Somewhere around 1900 new ways of refining sugar were invented, making sugar much less expensive. It got so almost anyone could afford to buy sugar—he didn't have to be rich.

During World War I sugar was scarce and interest in honey revived. It is interesting to note that Sir Arthur Conan Doyle, when he "retired" his famous detective-character, Sherlock Holmes, made him in his old age a beekeeper on the Sussex Downs. Beekeeping in America became popular and the use of honey increased. Farmers got good prices for their honey. Meanwhile, the mass-production techniques applied to producing war materials provided an incentive for mass production of consumer items. After the war these techniques were applied to packaging and marketing sugar. Sugar producers and distributors spent millions of dollars on advertising campaigns. Rich and poor alike began to use sugar almost to the complete exclusion of honey. Honey fell into the category of a luxury!

As often happens in styles of dress and styles of furniture and design there comes a time when people turn back and rediscover the past. That's what's happening now with honey.

Turning back or turning on to nature—it's all part of the present scene. And turning back to or rediscovering natural foods is part of it: nostalgia for the simple, honest life including simple, honest foods like honey.

Some sociologists say the turning back to nature may herald a new morality and honesty in society.

chpt 2

Who knows? Like health foods morality and honesty have always been with us. They never went anywhere—just got pushed aside in the frantic jangle of modern living.

Copy 7/1971

— chpt. 3 —
pg 29 to 35 ...
qre from

3

HONEY: HOW IT IS MADE

THE BEE COMMUNE

Honeybees work as nature's matchmakers in the fields, then come home to work as nature's honey-makers in a highly organized and directed society called the hive or colony. Each bee works for the good of the whole community in an atmosphere dominated and operated by females, who "control" population, sex of the "children," production of honey, distribution of work.

A colony of honeybees usually consists of a queen, a few hundred drones, and several thousand workers. The queen is the only fertile female, the drones are the only males, and the workers are *un*fertile females. The job of the queen is to lay eggs and maintain a harmonious atmosphere in the colony. The dominating impulse of the entire colony apparently is to insure the survival of the species rather than that of the individual. None of the three castes can live long through individual effort.

The queen is reared in a special cell that is usually suspended vertically from either the surface or the lower part of the honeycomb. She develops from the same kind of egg as the worker. Her queenly attributes come about because of the special diet of royal jelly she is fed by the workers.

According to poets the queen has one "mad moment of love," but according to authoritative texts she has several. Usually within five to ten days after leaving the queen cell, she takes one or more flights and mates with a drone while in the air. She may mate more than once before starting to lay eggs. The drone dies at the time of copulation. He's fulfilled his function in the commune and is no longer needed.

The queen returns to the hive filled with sperms stored in a special sperm sac inside her abdomen, called the spermatheca. From this she releases sperms "at will." If she fertilizes her eggs (that is, unites an egg with sperm), the result is a female. If she doesn't fertilize the egg, the result is a drone.

By some means of communication no one has yet figured out, the bees "control" their population. If they need more workers they produce more; if they need less, they produce less.

The drone is larger and heavier than the worker but shorter than the queen. He's the only kind of male bee in the colony and his sole function in life is to mate with the queen. He possesses no sting, nor does he have a pollen basket and wax glands like the worker. He depends on being fed by the workers. If he doesn't "make it" with the queen, he's pushed out of the hive to fend for himself, which he's not equipped to do. So the life of a drone after his eviction is brief.

Although the worker bee is female, she lacks the fully developed reproductive organs of the queen. Workers perform all the labor of the hive in a fairly definite routine. First, after emerging from the larval cell, they comb themselves and eat honey with pollen to gain strength for their tasks. After that, in successive periods, they clean out the cells, feed the older larvae and the younger larvae, take "orientation" flights, clean the hive, evaporate nectar, build honeycombs. Besides all that, they act as sentinels and "air conditioners" to provide the proper temperature for making honey.

After this period of home training they engage in field duties of carrying water, pollen, nectar, and *propolis*. (Propolis is a brownish resinous material of waxy consistency collected from the buds of trees. It's used for cement in building the honeycombs.)

Workers also serve as scouts. They search for new sources of nectar, pollen, and propolis. As Karl von Frisch has shown, scout bees "communicate" information to the colony members by dancing. The dance varies according to the direction of the sources and the distance required to reach them.

If food material is located within 50 to 100 yards of the hive the dancing bee circles in a narrow space, first to the left, then to the right, in the form of a figure 8, with her head toward the center of the figure. The greater the amount of food available, the greater will be the number of bees dancing.

When the source of supply is located beyond the 50 to 100 yard range, the scout bees perform a tail-wagging dance in which the bee first turns rapidly in a half circle, then moves in a given direction for a short distance, and then circles in the opposite direction, actively wagging her abdomen while traveling in a straight line.

The ingredients the bees collect to make their honey food are chosen to fill their specific needs. The pollen provides the protein absolutely essential to the growth of the larvae (eggs); the nectar provides the carbohydrates needed for performing energy-consuming tasks. Both the pollen and nectar provide minerals and other substances so vital to the diet.

Worker bees can live on honey or when necessary on syrup made from beet or cane sugar and, apparently, require little pollen except to rear the brood.

Nurse bees, who concoct the royal jelly fed to all larvae under two days of age and to the queen larvae during the entire feeding period, require honey, pollen, and water. When the worker and drone larvae are two days old, they are fed coarser food, consisting of honey and pollen mixed with brood food secreted by the food glands located in the head of the nurse bee.

For years, biologists, apiculturists—even psychologists and linguists—have been intrigued by the habits and life style of honeybees. Most particularly, they have been (and still are) intrigued by the "language" of the bees. Numerous experiments have been made and are still being made, and new information is made available from time to time concerning honeybees.

One of the most ardent students of honeybees, Karl von Frisch, studied bees for about forty-five years. He dissected and analyzed them in every way he could. He observed them inside and outside their hives. From his findings came the description of the bees' system of communication by dancing. He also described how the bee actually "processes" the nectar.

According to his observations, the fresh nectar brought in by the foraging bees is distributed among the worker bees. The worker bees, by regurgitation, expose droplets of the nectar to the warm air. (The temperature of the hive is maintained by the bees at around 95 degrees.) These manipulations cause much of the nectar's water to evaporate and the resulting substance thickens when the bees store it in the open cells.

The foregoing partially explains how the bees pre-digest the sugars contained in nectar, thereby making the honey sugars so easily assimilated by humans. But even von Frisch, with all his knowledge, studies, and observations, acknowledged an "unknown factor"—the factor that imparts to honey its health-giving and therapeutic qualities.

EXTRACTION OF THE HONEY

The honeycomb is completely departmentalized. It provides living quarters for each caste in their various stages of development, plus storage units for nectar, pollen, honey, and other "supplies." Functional in design, it's built to fill the needs of the bees in their communal endeavors.

Constructed by the bees from self-manufactured wax for utilitarian purposes, it's been called by artists and architects a "masterpiece of symmetry and beauty." Its design has been copied by man but never improved upon.

There's a story about a man who tried to duplicate a honeycomb and replaced the bees' natural one with his. They rejected it because it didn't work. It seems they construct the honeycomb with just enough "tip" in it so the honey will not spill out.

All honeycombs are identical in construction wherever they may be, although they may vary in size according to the requirements of the commune.

Wild bees build their hives in the hollows of trees, in the branches of trees, on wooden walls, in the eaves of a barn or a house. Domesticated bees live in hives built for them out of wood. The top of such a wooden hive may be opened and the combs removed when the honey is ripe for extraction. The beekeeper is able to look into the hive when he wishes. If he wants to move the colony he takes out the queen bee and the others attracted by her special scent, swarm around her.

Honey is extracted from the combs by a honey extractor, called a "honey machine." It operates by centrifugal force. The combs are first uncapped (the covering is removed) on both sides with an uncapping knife, which is heated by steam, electricity, or hot water. The uncapped combs are placed in the baskets of the extractor. At first the baskets are turned slowly until part of the honey is removed on one side; then they are reversed and the process is repeated. To remove all the honey requires an increase of speed, but not to the extent that the combs will be broken. Honey is easiest to extract before it loses the warmth of the hive.

The extracted honey runs from the extractor into a sump which allows the larger particles of comb to be separated from the honey before it goes through the honey pump or into the storage tanks. When a pump is not used, the honey is run through a coarse strainer to remove these particles. In cool weather, or with heavy honey, the liquid must be heated in a water-jacketed tank to facilitate straining. If heated to 110°F., the honey strains readily.

Air bubbles sometimes form at the top of the honey. They don't affect the quality of the honey, only its appearance. If honey is canned or bottled immediately after being extracted, the small bubbles form a white scum or foam on the surface. This, too, does not affect the quality of the honey, only its appearance.

(The above is the most popular method of extraction used by beekeepers. There are other methods.)

Essentially, man's method for extracting honey is the same today as it was in primitive times, except that in the early days of honey-gathering the beekeeper used smoke to expel the bees so he could remove the honeycombs. In some primitive lands, the smoking out method is still in use.

Honeybees haven't changed their methods—only their environment, from wild to domestic. Their social and working habits remain constant, as does the special something they contribute to honey. Their influence reaches far beyond the fields and the beehives.

- chpt. 4 -
goes from pg 37 to 44...

4

COMPOSITION OF HONEY

The composition of honey varies according to environmental conditions (chiefly relative humidity), floral source, ripeness when extracted, methods used in processing, and conditions of storage. There are hundreds of varieties of honey in the United States alone, and if you consider the world the varieties of honey number in the thousands! And floral sources, soil conditions, climatic conditions, would probably run into the tens of thousands!

CLIMATE

Climatic conditions vary within a state, even within a portion of a state. California, for example, the No. 1 producer of honey in the United States, boasts many variations of climate. You have northern California, central California, southern California. Within each of these areas are coastal, valley, mountain, desert regions. Break them down a little more and you have lower valley, upper valley, low desert, high desert, low mountain (foothills), high mountains. And even within this breakdown certain variables exist, for example as between the seaward and landward slopes of hills.

A tiny state like Vermont, or even larger states like Utah and Montana, don't have as many variables, but they do have some. (Anyone who's driven across the United States can attest to passing through half a dozen weather changes in one day!)

Degree of humidity in a given area influences the water content of honey. Honeys deriving from flowers grown in humid climates contain more moisture than those deriving from flowers grown in dry climates.

Soil content influences the composition of honey. Some soils are alkaline, others acid. Mineral content varies, so that the traces of potassium, ash, nitrogen, sulphur, manganese, and iron found in honey also vary.

But within this context there exist basic similarities among all honeys.

Honey contains certain enzymes and minerals difficult to demonstrate quantitatively. Honey also contains certain aromatic bodies.

Certain acids are found in honey. There are traces of phosphoric, citric, oxalic, tartaric, lactic, and acetic acids, among others. Especially in buckwheat honey, some tannic acid is also found; this is said to be the major cause for its dark color and stringent taste.

The following chart, prepared by the *American Honey Institute*, shows the average chemical composition of honey:

PRINCIPAL COMPONENTS	PER CENT
Water	17.7
Levulose (fruit sugar)	40.5
Dextrose (grape sugar)	34.0
Sucrose (cane sugar)	1.9
Dextrins and gums	1.5
Ash (silicon, iron, copper, manganese, chlorine, calcium, potassium, sodium, phosphorus, sulfur, aluminum, magnesium)	0.18
Total	95.78

(This leaves an undetermined factor of 4.22 per cent. It should also be noted that one teaspoon of extracted honey contains about 21 calories.)

Honey contains aroma and flavor substances which, in turn, contain essential oils. Also found in honey are minute amounts of enzymes and yeasts. The color substances of honey contain plant pigments, chlorophyll decomposition products, and colloidal particles.

Essentially, all the substances found in honey emanate from the soil and the chemical structure of the plants from which the bees obtain their nectar and pollen. To this must be added the special way in which the bees blend these substances to make the honey.

The mineral content of honey varies according to source. Highest mineral content appears in dark honeys, like buckwheat and heather, which have about four times as much iron as the light honeys, like clover, orange and sage.

Considerable controversy exists regarding the vi-~min content of honey. It's been shown that the ⌐   ⌐ many flowers contains a higher vitamin C content than almost any fruit or vegetable. Consequently, it has been assumed that the higher pollen content of honey the more vitamin C it contains.

But so many variables affect the ultimate vitamin content of honey that it is difficult to assess its actual vitamin content accurately. For example: Often the bees will consume nearly all of the pollen themselves and use only a small fraction in making the honey. Two batches of honey obtained from the same farmer from the same bees will differ. A hot, dry season or a cold, wet one in the area where the flowers were grown from which the honeybees gather nectar affects the vitamin content of honey.

Tests have been taken to determine the potential alkalinity of honey. On the basis of samples of representative American honeys it was found that the darker honeys had a higher alkaline level than the lighter ones, but that all honeys compared favorably with other alkaline foods.

Generally, the sugar content of honey runs between 70 and 80 percent.

Levulose (also called *fructose*) is similar to the sugar found in fruits.

Dextrose (also called *glucose*) is a type of sugar less sweet than cane sugar, occurring naturally in fruits and especially in grapes.

Sucrose is a crystalline sugar found in sugar cane and sugar beets.

Dextrin is a gummy substance which is an important factor in making honey easily digestible.

Following is a table prepared by the Department of Agriculture showing the dextrose and levulose content of representative honeys:

KIND OF HONEY	DEXTROSE	LEVULOSE
Tupelo	24.73%	48.61%
Sage	31.80	42.80
Apple	31.67	42.00
Alsike clover	36.06	40.95
Buckwheat	36.75	40.29
White clover	34.96	40.24
Alfalfa	36.85	40.24
Sweet clover	36.78	39.59

FLORAL SOURCE

Floral sources, important influences on the composition of honey, vary even more than climatic conditions. In the United States alone there are tens of thousands of flowers, some not even catalogued.

The floral source of honey determines its flavor and aroma. If bees gather nectar from orange blossoms, the honey will have the taste and aroma of oranges. If bees gather nectar from sage blossoms, the honey will have the taste and aroma of sage. If the bees gather from many sources, like a field of wildflowers, the flavor of the honey will be indeterminable, a mixture of many flavors.

The honeybee generally works on only one source at a time. A colony, however, may gather nectar from two or more sources before the surplus is extracted by the beekeeper, and thus produce a natural blend of two or more distinct flavors.

It's possible to provide relatively "controlled" sources for honeybees, but no one can guarantee that some of the bees might not stray. Beekeepers rent out colonies of bees to cross-pollinate crops to insure more vigorous plant reproduction. Alfalfa, an important crop in California, is grown over vast acreage. A farmer calls a beekeeper, asks for several colonies of bees; the beekeeper brings the colonies out and leaves them for several months.

In a situation like this the resulting honey would be *alfalfa* flavored and the chances of it being blended with any other flavor are slight. (Unless there's a field of clover across the road.)

The above is one example of a "controlled" source, insofar as floral aroma and flavor are involved. As a rule bees control the source, more or less, by returning to the same flower for nectar. If fields are covered with only one type of flowering plant, they'd more likely than not gather from that one source. A few stray bees going into another field wouldn't much alter the overall flavor or content of the honey.

RIPENESS

The *ripeness* of honey when the beekeeper removes the honeycombs from the beehive affects the composition of honey. Ripeness is determined by moisture content. If the moisture content is too high, the honey tends to ferment. Honey taken from uncapped combs has a higher moisture content than honey taken from capped combs.

Thoroughly ripened comb honey contains at its highest point about 16 to 17 percent moisture; at its lowest point about 13½ percent. Up to 18 percent moisture content is considered "safe." Well-ripened honey will not ferment unless it is exposed to a moist atmosphere long enough to absorb considerable moisture. Honey with a moisture content of less than 18 percent will seldom ferment if kept in airtight containers.

Honey handlers can test the moisture content of a batch of honey by use of a refractometer. The refractometer requires only a single drop of honey to determine moisture content. If moisture content goes to 19 percent and over the honey must be heated to a temperature of 145°F. for one hour. Yeasts in honey are killed by a temperature of 145°, and the honey will not ferment if kept in airtight containers.

(Honey will give off moisture in a dry, warm atmosphere, but will absorb moisture under humid conditions.)

Honeybees provide "airtight containers" in their storage cells and if beekeepers harvest only capped

44) — chpt. 4 —

honey the moisture content will be well below the
fermentation level.

Moisture content from the original nectar is high.
Honeybees carry the nectar in their honey-stomachs
until they return to the hive. While they're carrying the nectar, it undergoes certain "processing" in
the honey-stomach. Upon their return to the beehive worker bees transfer the nectar from the
honey-stomach to the honeycomb storage cells.
During the transferring procedure the nectar is further "processed" by the bees and undergoes certain
chemical changes.

Finally, the uncapped honey is "ventilated" by
means of incessant fluttering of wings of many
workers until the moisture is reduced to a "safe"
level. At that point, which the bees somehow seem
to judge precisely, the workers cap and seal the
honey by means of a wax covering they "manufac-
ture" from their wax glands.

The resulting honey is called comb-ripened
honey, and is considered to be the best type of
honey.

5

CHARACTERISTICS OF HONEY

Most people eat honey because it makes them feel good or because they just like it. Whatever characteristics honey possesses seem to be secondary.

Stored in honeycombs under natural beehive conditions honey is sheltered and protected, but when it goes out into the world it acts upon other substances and also reacts to them.

Generally speaking, honey reacts to changes in temperature and humidity. It also takes on certain characteristics, such as color, texture, and clarity or lack of clarity, by the way it is handled after it leaves the honeycombs.

But honey retains its basic health-giving qualities and purity despite any outward changes in its appearance.

Many erroneous ideas about honey's characteristics exist in the general populace. During interviews with the author, for example, several people said crystallized honey was spoiled. One woman said, "I throw the honey out when it turns sugary."

Others believed honey should be kept in the refrigerator. Some thought the honey was impure if it was cloudy. One very adamant middle-aged gentleman insisted honey was cooked with sugar and flavoring like jelly and jam. Quite a few believed the flavors—orange, sage, clover, alfalfa, etc.—were added to the honey.

An old-time country beekeeper told the author:

> I remember when nobody thought much about it. You just ate honey off the comb mostly 'cause it was good and it was handy. Then we started to send the stuff to the markets and you shoulda heard the holler! They'd be sendin' the stuff back 'cause it was full of sugar crystals, or foamy. Said the customers wouldn't buy. . . . Sure's lots of things city folk don't know 'bout honey!

Honey granulates (crystallizes) at temperatures ranging between 50° and 65°F. It also granulates with age. Granulation doesn't alter the content and flavor of honey in any way; it alters only its appearance.

Not all honeys are liquid. A few, like the Hawaiian *alergoba* honey, granulate quickly. In many European and Latin countries granulated honey is preferred over liquid honey and regarded as a delicacy.

Granulation in honey is caused by sugar crystals. Nearly all honeys granulate. How rapidly they will granulate depends on the proportions of levulose and dextrose content. Honeys high in levulose, like tupelo and sage, do not tend to granulate. But honeys high in dextrose, like alfalfa, clover, and buckwheat, form crystals fairly quickly. Packers who want to hasten the granulation of honey in order to sell it in solid chunks use the same technique employed by candymakers: stirring the honey until the crystals form. Stirring, or agitation, causes almost any honey high in dextrose to granulate rapidly.

A famous Russian sugar chemist discovered a method of reversing the process of crystallization, so that honeys high in dextrose would not granulate for long periods. He did this by removing the honey from the comb, straining it, slowly heating it to a temperature of 140° to 150°, and holding it at that point for about half an hour. With this method the tiny dextrose crystals which all honeys contain in varying percentages dissolved and did not readily reform. The flavor and bouquet of the honey was not altered.

Many American honey packers, who had a problem convincing American women that crystallized honey was not "bad," adopted the Russian technique.

Most labels on jars and cans of honey bear the legend: "This honey will crystallize. Crystallization doesn't impair the quality or flavor of the honey. Simply place the jar or can in a vessel of warm water and the honey will regain its liquidity."

Honey will crystallize if placed in the refrigerator. But it doesn't require refrigeration. It may be stored at room temperature. However, it should be covered because uncovered honey loses aroma and flavor and absorbs moisture and odors.

Another recommended method for reliquifying honey after it has granulated is to place the container in a pan of hot water and put it in the oven with a temperature control of no higher than 200°.

Honey is hygroscopic, which means it has the power to draw moisture out of the air or out of any moisture-bearing material—even a stone crock. This characteristic of honey makes it highly desirable in commercially baked cookies, cakes, and breads, which remain *naturally* fresh. They don't require artificial preservatives to keep them fresh. Most labels show the contents of cakes, breads, and cookies. If honey is used as a sweetener, the product will retain moisture almost indefinitely. Crackers and cookies baked with honey will be soft rather than crisp. If crisp cookies and crackers are desired, they may simply be heated in a slow oven before serving.

Bacteria will not live in honey.

Recently a group of bacteriologists conducted experiments to determine whether bacteria introduced into honey would survive. They chose various common disease organisms that afflict man. Within a few hours or a few days all the organisms died. The scientists claimed this was due to the hygroscopic nature of honey. A certain amount of moisture is necessary to maintain living organisms, including bacteria. The honey withdrew moisture from the bacteria and the bacteria died. (This bactericidal property of honey has been found to be separate from the high concentration of sugars.)

Honey may change color.

When stored over a period of years honey will become darker. This change is hastened if the honey is stored at higher than room temperature (which is about 70°F.).

Also, some honeys are less stable in this respect than others. Honeys which were originally white may become light amber or dark amber within five years, and the color will change to darker shades with the passage of time. Much of the original aroma and flavor will also be lost with increase in color.

Generally, a temperature of 145° to 160°F. for one hour will cause little change in color or flavor. This heat is suitable for all purposes of straining or liquifying honey. If the honey is heated in this manner and bottled at about 135°F., then quickly cooled, it will remain liquid longer than unheated honey.

It has been found that the enzymes and the bactericidal property of honey are reduced in value if the honey is heated to too high a temperature for too long a period. The safe amount of heat that can be applied varies with honeys from different floral sources.

Foods baked with honey brown faster and therefore require a lower oven temperature.

Honey will ferment under certain conditions.

Practically all honeys contain sugar-tolerant yeasts, derived chiefly from the nectar and pollen of flowers. Honeys that are not well ripened in the hive before extraction contain a higher moisture content and are, therefore, more readily affected by the action of yeasts.

Honey is generally thought to keep indefinitely, but recent investigations indicate that only when it is stored at 50°F. or below will it keep for a long period. At this temperature the sugar-tolerant yeasts are practically inactive. At temperatures around 60° granulated honey in particular is subject to fermentation and especially so if it has a moisture content of 19 percent.

Yeasts in honey are destroyed by a temperature of 145°F. for one hour. Honey heated to this point will not ferment if kept in airtight containers.

Well-ripened honey will not ferment unless it is exposed to a moist atmosphere long enough to absorb considerable moisture.

Honey that has less than 18 percent moisture will seldom ferment if kept in airtight containers.

Honey that has been diluted with water or other liquid may ferment or mold quickly if not kept cold. If honey has been diluted with any liquid, it should be refrigerated.

Honey packed in glass jars often appears cloudy. The cloudiness is caused by the pollen content and in no way affects the purity of honey. All honey is pure.

Often there is a thin whitish film, or foam, on the surface of the honey, which also in no way impairs the honey. This happens in the pouring process.

At the bottom of a jar or can, honey seems to thicken. This is a normal condition and doesn't alter the content of the honey.

Despite its reactions in the world of foods and atmospheric variables with which it mingles, honey always retains its nutritive, health-giving qualities—and its spark of magic!

6

VARIATIONS AND CLASSIFICATIONS

Varieties of honey number almost as many as the flowers from which honeybees gather nectar.

A recent check of a large Los Angeles market revealed the following varieties: Alfalfa, Avocado, Buckwheat, Orange, Sage, Eucalyptus, Tupelo (Blossom Honey), Safflower, Yucatan Wild Jungle Honey (from jungle blossoms), California Orange Honey, Texas Grapefruit Honey, Utah Alfalfa Honey, Colorado Alfalfa Honey, Wild Honey, Biblical Honey. According to honey authorities this is a small sampling of the hundreds of varieties that exist in the United States alone, not counting all the honeys from foreign lands!

Honey falls into two major classifications: extracted honey and comb honey.

Extracted honey is the liquid honey separated from the comb. It's packed in jars or tin containers.

As a rule the lightest colored honeys are the mild-est. Well over half the honey produced in the United States is light-colored, mild-flavored. Sweetclover, clover, and alfalfa are examples of light-colored honeys. Buckwheat honey is probably the darkest.

Comb honey is sold as section-comb, cut-comb, and chunk honey. Section-comb honey comes in the wooden frames in which the bees stored the honey, usually weighs just under a pound. The wooden sections may be in paper or cardboard cartons or in transparent wrappers.

Cut-comb honey has been taken out of the frames, cut in pieces and each piece wrapped sep-arately.

Chunk honey consists of pieces of comb honey in a container with liquid honey filled in around them.

Both extracted honey and comb honey are sold in granulated form.

California is the top-ranking honey producing state in the United States and is famous for sage, alfalfa, orange-blossom, and star-thistle honeys. The other honey-producing states are in every part of the country: Michigan, Ohio, Wisconsin, Illinois, Iowa, Texas, Minnesota, Colorado, Utah, Montana, Washington, Oregon, the New England states. Florida is famous for its tupelo honey.

Honeys of the northern states tend to be some-what sweeter and thicker than those of the south-ern regions. Southern areas in the United States seem to be better suited for raising bees for sale than for producing honey.

The largest honey yield comes from areas with the heaviest nectar crops, such as alfalfa, alsike clover, sweet clover, and white clover. These crops are most abundant in the northern states and in California.

Honeybees prefer to gather nectar in hot dry weather rather than cool or rainy weather. The hotter the weather the busier they are. There are about eighteen hundred kinds of plants, trees, and shrubs in the United States from which bees gather nectar—and about 37,000 nectar loads go into the production of one pound of honey.

Bees rented out to farmers for cross-pollination account for a small amount of honey produced commercially, though their nectar sources would probably produce an interesting honey. For example, they pollinate asparagus, broccoli, brussels sprouts, cabbage, carrots, cauliflower, kale, onions, peppers, pumpkins, radishes, rutabagas, squash, turnips, to name a few. (An Ecuadorian friend told the author about delicious "onion honey" from his native land.)

An exception to the above is alfalfa honey. Alfalfa crops in California rank first in the United States. Most of the large alfalfa fields in California are pollinated by "rented" bees which in turn produce a delicious honey.

Honey produced in the United States is classified and graded according to federal and state standards. In California the Honey Standards Board exercises certain controls to insure compliance with federal and state standards.

Comb honey is graded according to the weight, cappings, cleanliness, and fullness of the combs. (Cleanliness means absence of bee particles, wood slivers, or other foreign substances.)

The federal standards divide the grades into U.S. Fancy, U.S. No. 1, and U.S. No. 2. The principal differences between these three grades are the appearance of the honey and the fullness of the combs.

Federal standards for grades of extracted honey are based, primarily, on a score that includes consideration of flavor, absence of defects, clarity, and moisture content. The grades specified are:

U.S. Grade A or U.S. Fancy: This is considered top grade. It must contain not less than 81.4 percent soluble solids, with a moisture content not more than 18.6 percent. It must score not less than 90 points for flavor, absence of defects, and clarity. Most important in grading honey is flavor with respect to the predominating floral essence or floral blend. Absence of defects ranks next in importance. Also considered, but to a lesser extent, is clarity—that is, freedom from air bubbles, pollen grains, or other fine particles.

U.S. Grade B or U.S. Choice: This grade must also contain not less than 81.4 percent soluble solids and have a moisture content of not more than 18.6 percent. It must score not less than 80 points for flavor, absence of defects, and clarity.

(These two grades are the only ones found on retail market shelves.)

LABELING

Each label (on a retail package) should include the name of the contents, net weight, grade, color (when in an opaque or tin container), and the name and address of the packer. If the floral source is mentioned, the contents of the container must be true to that source.

The label on a five-gallon can of wild honey purchased recently by the author in a Los Angeles market bears the following legend:

This fine honey is gathered by the bees from many different wild flowers and plants that are native to our California deserts, such as mesquite, smoke tree, palo verde, greasewood, rabbit brush, ocotillo blooms, and many others.

Because of the dryness and high temperatures, this desert honey is very low in moisture, and high in minerals which are so essential to good nutrition.

This pure honey comes to you uncooked, unfiltered and unblended.

This honey will granulate. To liquify, place can in warm water. Remove lid. Heat slowly.

Following is a list of some of the trade terms found on honey labels in California markets:

Classified	Unfiltered
Unclassified	Filtered
Blended	Uncooked
Unblended	Unprocessed
Raw	Pure—100% Pure
Organic	

Briefly, this is what they mean in honey language:

Unclassified and Classified

Both these terms apply only to comb honey.

Unclassified indicates combs in which some of the cells are uncapped and empty. (For reasons known only to the bees some cells are left empty.)

Classified indicates that all combs are capped.

There's no difference in the quality or taste of the two honeys.

Blended and Unblended

Blended means that the nectar derives from many sources and has been blended by the bees like the wild honey described on the label reprinted above.

Blended may also mean honeys blended by the honey handler. Blending of honeys often results in subtler flavors and aromas than those found in single-source honeys. Also, from the honey handler's point of view, blending is preferable because he is able to control the flavor somewhat. In natural one-source (*unblended*) honey, variations in flavor occur. For example, one orange-blossom honey may have a rich flavor because of a period of sunny dry weather and another may have a weak, flat flavor because of a period of damp, cold weather. The honey handler may blend in some clover or sage to improve the flavor.

Many honey users prefer blended honeys, because of the subtler flavors.

Filtered and Unfiltered

Filtered honey has been filtered through certain types of filters which remove pollen grains and clarify the honey. To many consumers it is aesthetically more appealing than unfiltered honey. It generally costs more and has a beautiful clear transparent appearance.

Unfiltered honey is cloudy in appearance. Cloudiness in unfiltered honey is primarily caused by the presence of pollen grains. Many consumers (particularly those interested in health foods) prefer unfiltered honey because it retains the original nature-given ingredients.

Unprocessed

To the average consumer the term *processed* implies food that has been tampered with or changed in some way from its original natural form. It implies artificial treatment of one kind or another—something taken out, something added.

Honey contains no additives, nothing artificial. However it is handled it remains a *natural* unprocessed food.

Uncooked

Jams, jellies and preserves are cooked to thicken their juices. Honey is naturally thick and syrupy. It requires no cooking to give it the consistency of syrup.

No honey is "cooked" in the sense that other foods are cooked, to break down the fibers or tissues as in meats and vegetables. Honey is often heated in water-jacketed containers to reduce it to a liquid state, but it isn't cooked.

Organic

The term *organic* applied to honey may be defined briefly as follows: Since the bee is a natural organism and all honey is made by bees all honey is *organic*.

To retailers and consumers the term "organic" implies the honey was obtained from the nectar of "organically grown" plants or in a completely natural environment unaltered by man.

One honey distributor interviewed by the author, put it this way: "To me, *organic* means honey from flowers grown the way God meant them to grow—free and wild. Take whatever comes, rain, sun, draught, cold, heat, whatever. That's organic."

Raw Honey

Raw honey means honey which is as close to its original natural state as possible.

Applied to honey, *raw* doesn't have the same meaning as it does when applied to meat. For example, raw meat is uncooked meat—usually inedible for human beings. It must be cooked first before it's eaten, by boiling, roasting, broiling, etc. Honey is ready to eat "as is."

Honey in capped combs could be called as close to the natural state as possible. It's just the way the bees eat it.

Raw honey may be purchased in capped combs, in chunks and in liquid form. The liquid form would contain everything but the combs.

Labeling is done by the honey distributors who tend to be very careful about what they put on the label so it conforms to the contents. Government inspectors, on both the state and national level, without notice, visit beekeepers, honey storerooms, (even retail stores) and pull a jar or can of honey off the shelf to check the accuracy of the labeling. They test samples in their laboratories and if they find that the contents do not coincide with the label they "red tag" the honey. (This means it cannot be sold.)

Pure

"Honey is pure whether or not it is stated on the label." So states a brochure from the California Honey Advisory Board.

No bacteria can live in honey, honey contains no additives, preservatives or adulterants. Honey is 100% pure!

HONEY FROM FOREIGN LANDS

Honey is international. And the same climatic variations govern production and composition whatever its source. Weather variables within a state or a region of a country affect not only the composition and production of honey but also the world honey market. In some instances abnormal weather wreaks particular havoc, with anticipated honey harvests and a country cannot produce enough honey to meet its domestic demand and its export commitments.

An article in a current publication mentions that due to a prolonged cold, wet spell, France was importing honey from Mexico. In Southern California the lack of sufficient rain during the winter of 1970-71 curtailed the spring honey harvest. The United States in that year (1970) imported almost as much honey as it exported.

Honey is a world-trade commodity. Each country tries to maintain high standards in its honey production to make its honey attractive to foreign buyers.

Mexican honey, particularly honey from Yucatan, is considered excellent. So are the honeys from Canada and England.

France also takes great pride in its honeys. Some experts claim that because of the special chemical nature of the soil in many regions of France where honey is produced, French honey is superior. Acres of jasmine flowers grown at Grasse in France, for perfume-making, are the source of a world-renowned honey. Narbonne, one of the old provinces of France, produces a crystal white, granular and highly aromatic honey. Rosemary honeys are among France's best. The French prize a special sea-green honey, made from the blooms of gooseberry bushes and sycamore trees.

Greek honeys, from the "land of the gods," are considered superb. One of the best-known honeys for sale in American markets, called Hymettus, derives from the blossoms on Mt. Hymettus near Athens. It has a deep greenish-amber tone and a delicate flavor of thyme.

Scotland is famous for its heather honey. It's extremely thick, highly aromatic, and somewhat purplish. Because of its unusual mineral content doctors often recommend its use to convalescents.

A famous "international" honey, considered to be one of the finest in the world, is the guajillo honey of Texas. It is water-white, with a delicate milky tone, and comes from an acacia shrub native to southeastern Texas.

Imported honeys are available at gourmet shops or in specialty ethnic food departments. Most of them bear no grading or classification—merely the source, the packer, and the weight. It's safe to assume that all foreign honeys that reach the shelves of markets in the United States are of superior quality.

Honeys vary in color from the water-white of Texas guajillo honey to the black honeys of Brazil, with shades of amber in between ranging from pale yellow to deep green-gold. They vary in flavor and aroma from the mild sea-green honey of France to the pungent spicy honeys of the West Indies. There's a taste of honey for everyone's taste, and no matter what its origin there is the bees' own special magic—a magic that crosses na-

chpt 6

(61)

tional and international boundaries, language differences, even political differences. (Mainland
China, which at this writing contributes large
quantities of honey to the world market, though
not a member of the United Nations, is a "member" of the international honey market.)

7

HONEY IN HISTORY

PREHISTORIC HONEY

Prehistoric man, looking to nature for his survival, learned from observation and experiment—and some of his observation he recorded.

Most probably life in the Stone Age was communal, similar to life in the beehive. And, like the female worker bees, prehistoric females bore children and cared for them, cleaned, prepared food.

Unlike the drone of the bee community, the male of the human species served a broader purpose than procreation. He was the explorer, the searcher for food, the hunter, even the artist.

For reasons no one really knows, prehistoric man painted on the walls of caves. He recorded some of his daily activities. Archaeologists believe he did this in ceremonies conducted before the hunt for purposes of magic. He may have believed, for example, that by painting a picture of a man spearing a bison, he would absorb some magical power that would guarantee his success in hunting down a bison the following day.

One such drawing found on the walls of a cave in northern Spain depicts a man climbing a stone cliff with the help of some ropes. He's reaching for a beehive high in the rocks, and figures of bees flutter around him. This drawing is said to date back some twenty thousand years.

In drawing this scene, the artist may have projected a "wish" or he may have recorded something he saw. But it's apparent from the drawing that primitive man knew about honey and bees. What compelled him to climb the rocky cliff (or think about climbing the cliff) to reach for a beehive remains a mystery. He may have felt a drop of honey "falling from the sky" and, being naturally curious, sought out its source; or he may have observed an animal rob a beehive and decided to find out what there was to discover.

Besides cave drawings the only other records historians and achaeologists have to "reconstruct" the life of primitive man consist of artifacts or adornments uncovered in archaeological digs. One such find, perhaps worn or carried as jewelry, and discovered in a region of Central Europe, is some fossilized amber in which is embedded a bee, of the same size and with the same structure as a modern honeybee.

Other evidence of the use of honey by primitive man in the Neolithic period was discovered in the ancient lake dwellings of Switzerland. This evidence consists of vessels used for straining honey, similar to vessels still in use by natives of that area.

It is believed that in addition to obtaining honey from wild bees, primitive man domesticated the bees just as he tamed horses, oxen and sheep.

It's assumed he used honey mainly as a food. So far nothing has been uncovered to indicate that he used it for ceremonial or medicinal purposes, although archaeologists believe it's quite likely he did. They base this belief on the fact that in many existing primitive societies in Africa, New Guinea, New Zealand, South America, honey is used in religious rites. And, from a behavioral standpoint, primitive man of two hundred centuries B.C. and primitive man of twenty centuries A.D. are thought to be almost identical.

HONEY IN ANCIENT EGYPT

Egypt, in the fertile valley of the Nile (sometimes called the cradle of civilization), embraced honey and the honeybee in everyday life, in love, in ceremonies, from birth to death. The bee "motif" appears in designs, carvings, drawings, in jewelry, in textiles. The figure of a bee sat next to the signature of a pharaoh on official papers. Lower Egypt, that is, Egypt of the Nile Delta, was known as the "land of the bee."

Egyptians meticulously recorded every facet of their daily activities, and mention of honey as a food, as a symbol, as a means of exchange, as a harbinger of good fortune, health and glory, appears on numerous tablets and papyri.

Drawings found on the walls of tombs and inscribed on temple walls portrayed the orderly lifestyle of the ancient Egyptian, a life-style reflected in the geometric precision of Egyptian architecture and dress. Daily records were kept by tax collectors and by the "bookkeepers" of the day. To the ruling class of Egypt the organization, industry, perseverance and efficiency of the bee symbolized the epitome of the well-ordered life to which it aspired. Slaves were exhorted to follow the example of the honeybee.

A detailed description of Egyptian beekeeping comes from a bas-relief in a temple at Abusir and dates back to about 2500 B.C. It shows the use of a smoker to subdue the bees so the honeycomb could be removed. The smoker appears to be fashioned of pottery, and a beekeeper is blowing smoke through it into the hive. The hives seem to be made from cylindrical pipes piled up in rows. (The same type of hive may be found in use in some parts of Egypt today.) Also shown is honey being extracted from the comb, filtered, and packed into jars.

Evidence that ancient Egyptians blended industry with pleasure comes from their numerous drawings of dancing, music-making, and feasting. Feasting, naturally, called for drinking. And the ancient Egyptians were noted as great beer drinkers. They concocted a brew from wheat, barley, and honey, similar to the Roman and British mead of later years.

In Egyptian medicines honey and milk were used extensively. Sacrifices to Egyptian deities were made with honey. Visiting dignitaries often brought gifts of honey to Egyptian kings and princes. A gift of honey from a lover or betrothed signified constancy and devotion. To the Egyptians all the attributes of the honeybee were embodied in the honey, plus whatever extra magic the bee added—a magic that made honey so popular in wedding ceremonies and religious ceremonies.

No mention is made in history books as to

whether or not Cleopatra enticed Antony with Egyptian honey coupled with her own charms, but it's not improbable, since gifts of honey were common in a lover relationship.

Beekeeping is still popular in modern Egypt and Egyptian honey is considered some of the world's finest.

HONEY IN ANCIENT GREECE

To the ancient Greeks, honey had a special significance. Honey, an ingredient of the food and drink of the gods, ambrosia and nectar, became almost synonymous with youth, vitality, and longevity. Greek gods possessed all the vices and virtues of their human counterparts. They partook freely of earthly pleasures, among which love-making and feasting ranked high.

Imaginative writers compared Greece to "a sensitive hand, its delicate fingers tapering into the blue waters of the Mediterranean." On one of these sensitive fingers high in the rocky crags of its rugged mountains, wild honeybees also consorted. One of the most famous honeys of ancient Greece came from Mount Hymettus near Athens. Even today honey from Mount Hymettus may be purchased in food markets in the United States. Another famous Greek honey is made from the nectar of roses.

Greek scholars and poets wrote prolifically, and in their writings they extolled the virtues of honey. Honey from Attica, one of the states of ancient Greece in the vicinity of Athens, drew special praise for its medicinal and nutritional attributes.

The ancient Greeks glorified the body and mind. Any food that contributed to the enhancement of health, beauty and wisdom, enjoyed great popularity. Honey was fed freely to their great athletes and warriors.

The Greeks do not appear to have extolled the virtue and industry of the bee with the same fervor as the Egyptians. To the Greeks freedom of the individual ranked higher than communal efficiency. This freedom didn't extend to the slaves (who were expected to emulate the bees), but only to the free Greek citizens.

Records indicate that at the time of Pericles (just before 400 B.C.) twenty thousand hives existed in Attica.

Honey still comes from the slopes of Mount Hymettus just as it did in the time of Pericles, and honey in Greece is still referred to as *ambrosia*.

HONEY IN ANCIENT ROME

The historians say that the ancient Romans were a lusty, pleasure-seeking people who lived and loved with great gusto. Stories of Roman revelry are legion.

Romans also had a reputation for being great beekeepers and honey was a popular, everyday food. No menu was said to be complete without some dish or drink mixed with honey.

The vast Roman Empire encompassed many farmers and beekeepers. Each honey harvest called for a celebration, and since there were numerous variations of climate from one end of the Empire to the other, honey harvests occurred more than once a year. In some warm regions flowers bloomed in abundance practically all year and beekeepers harvested honey in the spring, summer, autumn, even in the winter.

The harvests heralded grand bouts of feasting, drinking and love-making. Honey flowed freely—as drink and as food. A special drink of the day was a mixture of honey, milk and poppy juice which is said to have induced a state of euphoria—good cheer and dizzy optimism followed by sleep and marvelous dreams! This was a favorite drink at wedding parties, where the bride and bridegroom were encouraged to imbibe freely. One goblet of this special brew insured marital bliss—at least in the nuptial bed!

Among the ruling classes magnificent banquet halls served as settings for feasting and revelry but honey drinks flowed as freely as they did among the peasants in the fields. Succulent foods were prepared in honey, served on enormous trays carried by slaves. Huge vats of honey brew were rolled in, poured into pitchers, then served in ornate beakers to speech-parched senators and their minions. (Ancient Romans had a reputation for oratory.)

Like the Egyptians and the Greeks, Romans used honey in libations to their gods. They also believed honey possessed "magic" powers to endow people with the genius of poetry and eloquence.

As a medium of barter and exchange honey was an important commodity. Peasants paid their taxes in honey and bought essential foods and farm implements with honey. Snails especially raised for Roman banquets were fattened and sweetened with honey.

Beekeeping still is a recognized occupation in

modern Rome—Italy. Italy is known for its fine honeys and for the *Italian* Queen Bee, a special breed of queen sold on the bee market. Some beekeepers prefer buying and introducing "foreign" queens into their hives, and the Italian queen is considered one of the best.

HONEY IN OTHER ANCIENT LANDS

In ancient times the British Isles were referred to as the Isles of Honey, a paradise of wild flowers and a haven for the honeybee. Long before Britain was conquered by the Romans, honey and beekeeping were well-established there. Welsh and Celtic legends antedating the Roman occupation are filled with stories about sparkling mead and honey drinks.

Tributes were paid with mead and honey. While there is evidence that honey was used for cooking and baking, its principal use seems to have been in the preparation of alcoholic drinks. From ancient times England seems to have been literally drenched in ale.

Ale is said to have originated with the Saxons. It was originally not a malt liquor but "made with honey or the washings of honeycombs." During the Danish invasion of England the word "ale" developed from the Danish word "öl," the term used to describe Danish *meth*. The ancient Danes and Teutons were reputed to be great drinkers of ale or mead.

Beekeeping and honey production were popular in all the European countries, and among Slavic people in particular. They used honey freely in their foods, mixed it with curds and butter, and made alcoholic drinks with honey. The Poles had a reputation for being the brewers of the finest mead. Many legends have been written about the enormous honeycombs found in Poland. One fable tells about a huge bear who fell into a honeycomb and drowned before he could be recovered or find a means of escape.

HONEY IN EARLY AMERICA

Up to the seventeenth century no honeybees existed on the American continent. They were brought to America by settlers from England, Spain, Holland, and France. The first traces of bees in the United States are found in Boston in about 1644; they are said to have been brought over by some Englishmen.

Once settled in the Americas the bees traveled and multiplied rapidly. They followed the pioneers in their treks west, and often preceded the human trail-breakers. From the Atlantic to the Pacific honeybees swarmed and colonized.

American Indians referred to the bees as "white man's flies," because their appearance heralded the arrival of the "pale-face intruders." Consequently, bees never became too popular with the American Indians.

In the year 1859 four swarms of bees were transported by a group of pioneers in a covered wagon from Boston to California. Along the way the bees were released from their hives and allowed to gather nectar—thus providing food for themselves and for the pioneers en route.

Early Texans described their honey as "the sweetest honey in the whole wide world." The greatest numbers of bees remained where the climate was dry and hot during the summer months. Southern California provided a wonderful haven for them.

During pioneer days in America, backwoodsmen made a business of selling wild honey which they gathered in the forests. Described in literature as a picturesque character with old sombrero, open hickory shirt and deerskin breeches, the honey-hunter generally settled on the banks of a river so he could paddle his honey to market by boat. His equipment consisted of several buckets, an axe, a fishing outfit, and a rifle as protection against bears, who themselves have a reputation as seekers-out of honey.

The honey-hunter often used honey as a means of exchange to obtain flour, gunpowder, and other necessities for his living. Those who traveled along the banks of the Mississippi sold honey to skippers of steamboats who, in turn, resold it at a profit when they reached New Orleans.

In foods, in drink, in medicine, in magic, in rituals and in trade, honey has served man well all through ancient and historic times. It could almost be said that the history of honey is the history of man.

copper — 1971

goes from pg. 73 to 80 incl.

8

HONEY IN RELIGION

In primitive religions offerings and sacrifices to
the gods are a common practice. Most of these religious ceremonies involved prayers supplemented
with gifts given to win favor with the gods, ap-
pease their anger, express gratitude, or to ward off
evil spirits. Sacrifices fell into categories of sin offerings or thanks offerings.

Farmers sacrificed fruit and harvest products or
animals like sheep, cattle, and horses. Hunters sacrificed their prey. In some countries even women
and children were sacrificed.

Honey occupies a special niche in the history of
"offerings." When certain people wanted to offer
something particularly acceptable or desirable to a
deity they offered honey, as an expression of pen-
itence, in atonement or thanksgiving. A graphic

picture of varieties of offerings comes from the
writings of the Greek, Sophocles, who wrote:

> Wool of the sheep was there, fruit of the vine,
> Libations and the treasured store of grapes
> And manifold fruits were there, mingled with
>   grain
> And oil of olive, and fair curious combs
> Of wax, compacted by the yellow bee.

Almost without exception the ancients regarded
honey as a symbol of love, wisdom, and purity.
During certain religious ceremonies honey was
poured on the hands to keep them pure from everything that causes pain or defilement. Honey was
believed to purify the tongue from every sin, to impart eloquence.

Sun-worshipping was common among primitive
people. The sun represented the most glorious ob-
ject of nature—a supreme god. Honey played a sig-
nificant part in rituals, the sun dances and libations.
The custom of honey offerings to the sun existed among the Egyptians, the Incas, and other
peoples. The Assyrians and Babylonians poured
honey on the foundation stones and walls of their
temples to insure the benevolence of the gods.
Priests anointed themselves with honey and placed
jars of honey on the altars of the gods. Honey sacrifices in beautiful vessels were carried to the temples before sunrise as an offering to the sun god.

Persians and Hindus used honey, considered a
sacred substance, profusely in their religious ser-
vices. Among present-day primitive societies in
Africa honey is still used in many rituals. The Hot-
tentots treat honey with particular reverence. Religious ceremonies are conducted before the taking
of the honey. No one is allowed to harvest honey

before a certain time indicated by the priests, who first taste the honey.

Two of the major religions of the Western World—Judaism and Christianity—were born in the eastern Mediterranean region where honey was plentiful. Little wonder that the Bible contains numerous references to honey and the use of honey in religious ceremonies.

The reference to Palestine as a land flowing with milk and honey is repeated numerous times in the Old Testament. The book of Samuel portrays the plentitude of honey:

> And all the people came into the forest; and there was honey upon the ground. And when the people were come into the forest, behold a flow of honey . . .
>
> *—Masoretic text*
> *I Sam. 14:25, 26*

Another, in the book of Job:

> He shall not see the rivers, the floods, the brooks of honey and butter . . .
>
> *—King James version*
> *Job 20:17*

The "heaven-sent manna" which sustained the Israelites during their wandering in the desert contained honey. Reference is made in Exodus:

> . . . And the house of Israel called the name thereof Manna; and it was like coriander seed, white; and the taste of it was like wafers made with honey.
>
> *—Masoretic text*
> *Ex. 16:31*

The Song of Songs, one of the books of the Old Testament, contains many allusions to honey. Ascribed to King Solomon (who had a reputation for being a great lover), it abounds with passages of tender emotion and sensual pleasure. It's generally considered to contain some of the most beautiful love lyrics ever written. According to the Jews, the lover is God and the bride is Israel; and according to the Christians the lover is Christ and the bride is the Church. But from the context of the poems it is possible they were simply love songs, perhaps sung by young lovers.

One of the passages reads as follows:

While the king sat at his table,
My spikenard sent forth its fragrance
My beloved is unto me as a cluster of henna
In the vineyards of En-gedi.
Behold, thou art fair, my beloved, yea, pleasant;
Also our couch is leafy.
The beams of our houses are cedars,
And our panels are cypresses.
>   —*Masoretic text*
>   *Song of Songs 1:12-17*

Another:

How fair is thy love, my sister, my bride!
How much better is thy love than wine!
And the smell of thine ointments than all manner of spices!
Thy lips, O my bride, drop honey—
Honey and milk are under thy tongue;
And the smell of thy garments is like the smell of Lebanon.
>   —*Song of Songs 4:10, 11*

Honey was frequently used in a symbolical sense, to draw a comparison between some act or concept and the sweetness of honey. In the Psalms of David the following passages occur:

The judgment of the Lord is sweeter than honey and the droppings of the honeycomb.

How sweet are thy words unto my taste! yea, sweeter than honey in my mouth.
>   *—King James version*
>   Ps. 119:103

In Solomon's Proverbs (5:3) is found the following:

Pleasant words are as an honeycomb, sweet to the soul and health to the bones.
For the lips of a strange woman drop as an honeycomb, and her mouth is smoother than oil.
>   *—Proverbs 16:24*

The Bible contains two accounts of men being ordered to eat a book, and in each instance reference is made to the book tasting "sweet as honey." (Ezek. 3:33, and Apoc. 10:9, 10.)

Sacrifices made with honey were forbidden by the Jews, as honey was liable to ferment. The phrase in the Bible reads: " ... ye shall burn no leaven, nor any honey in any offering of the Lord made by fire." (Lev. 2:11) As a "not burnt" offering or as a tribute of first fruit, honey offerings were allowed.

The Talmud mentions honey often. In one place a warning is given not to allow mustard plants to grow near bees' nests because bees partaking of their nectar might burn their throats. The Jews, forbidden to do work of any kind on the Sabbath, were given special dispensation to cover the bees in case of a heavy rain or scorching sun.

Many references are made in the Bible as to the use of honey as a gift. When Jacob sent his son to Egypt he gave him spices, myrrh, almonds, and honey to present to the governor.

When Jeroboam's queen visited the blind prophet Ahijah at Shiloh she brought with her a cruse of honey as a gift. By bringing honey she hoped to obtain a favorable report about her dying son and, also, she may have brought the honey to cure the prophet's blindness.

During the early days of Christianity a cup of honey and milk was given to neophytes in the baptismal ceremony. Later the practice was discontinued, but the Copts and Ethiopians continued to use honey in their baptismal ceremonies. In Ethiopia, too, the wine of communion is prepared from honey.

Before fast-days, especially on Holy Thursday, the Christians ate honey. On the eve of the Jewish New Year an apple dipped in honey was eaten.

Ancient Christian archives contain much to indicate the importance of bees, honey and wax in the Christian religion. One manuscript found in the Vatican library gives an interesting example: a supplication to the Lord to protect the bees, these "dear animals."

Before the main altar of St. Peter's Church in Rome is a huge bronze baldachin which is studded with figures of bees. Some authorities claim the shape of the papal tiara was derived from the old-fashioned beehive. Often the customs and orders of the Holy Church were compared to the bees.

Liturgical parchment manuscripts were illustrated with elaborate drawings of bees at work, in the hive, gathering nectar, making honey. In many cases the bees were used to portray humans working and serving the Church.

The food given to Christ by his disciples on the day he rose from the dead consisted of broiled fish and honeycomb. When John the Baptist was wandering through the wilderness he ate dried locusts and honey.

The purity and sweetness of honey have made it a symbol of the work of God and the ministry of Christ. Paradise, the reward of the faithful in their labors for Christ, is known as "the land of milk and honey," as the land of Canaan was in the Old Testament.

The bee, because of its industrious habits, has become the symbol of activity, diligence, work, and good order. Also, because the bee produces honey, she has come to be accepted as a symbol of sweetness and religious eloquence. The beehive is a recognized attribute in the art and iconography of St. Ambrose and of St. Bernard de Clairvaux, for their eloquence is said to have been as sweet as honey.

St. Ambrose (one of the four Latin Fathers of the Church) is often shown in paintings with a beehive—a reference to the legend that when he was an infant a swarm of bees alighted on his mouth, thus foretelling his future eloquence. St. Bernard is also shown with a beehive, as a symbol of his eloquence.

The beehive is the symbol of a pious and unified community. St. Ambrose compared the Church to a beehive, and the Christian to the bee, working ardently and forever true to the hive. As a producer of honey, which is a symbol of Christ, and for the virtue of its habits, the bee has been used to symbolize the virginity of Mary.

chpt. 8

Since, according to ancient legend, the bee never sleeps, it is occasionally used to suggest Christian vigilance and zeal in acquiring virtue.

For many years the ancient land of "milk and honey" lay fallow, buried in sand and covered with rocks. But the cradle of three religions is fast becoming a prolific mother. In their cooperative settlements (kibbutzim) Israelis aspire to show the world how people can work together for the common good. The Israeli kibbutz is very much like a beehive—everyone works to the best of his ability and everyone receives according to his needs.

Today in modern Jerusalem three of the world's major religions—Judaism, Christianity, and Islam—live in close juxtaposition, and honey once more flows. Israel, the new state, is proud of her honey and exports much of it to foreign markets. Special courses are given in agricultural schools to train beekeepers and great care is taken to keep the quality of Israeli honey superior.

chpt 9 —
pre fm pg. 81 to 90ııı

9

HONEY AS A HEALER

The successful use of honey as a healer for many
unhappy human or animal conditions, both physical and mental, has occurred in so many different
places, among so many different people at so many
different times that it falls outside the realm of
mere coincidence. It cannot be sloughed off as an
old wives' tale.

The practices of folk medicine are rarely recorded in professional medical journals. It's a people-
to-people "practice of medicine" no different today
than it was in the days of Julius Caesar. Some individual members of the medical profession are looking at the so-called home remedies with new eyes.
It's not uncommon in the modern world for a doctor to resort to an old-fashioned remedy when all
conventional, traditional methods of treatment fail.

A construction worker told the author that when

he was a young man he suffered terribly from poison oak. He lived in Northern California and farmed some land wth his brothers. "Every year I used to break out something awful," he said. He went to several doctors and everything they prescribed gave him only temporary relief. Finally, one doctor told him to "get a nanny goat, let the nanny goat eat the poison oak, and drink nanny goat milk." It seems nanny goats love to eat poison oak. By drinking its milk the young man immunized himself against poison oak.

The doctor may have had a similar experience with poison oak, or he may have known of someone who did, heard about the remedy, knew that it worked, and passed it on to the young man.

Some remedies are a result of "thinking out" a solution. A neighbor of the author told her that when he was a little boy in Pennsylvania he used to fight with his younger brother and chase him into the poison ivy. "You see," he said, "the poison ivy didn't bother me, I could roll around in it all day—but my brother used to break out all over!"

His mother cooked poison ivy leaves in water until she had a strong brew which she fed to his brother, and the rash disappeared. She said she figured it might work because she'd "heard about primitive natives somewhere who injected some kind of snake poison into themselves to make themselves immune to snake bites."

Today people buy their medications in bottles or jars, ready-made or prescription. Years ago (and even now in rural areas) people found their medications and cures in their natural surroundings and they learned by practice and observation. From trees and plants they took leaves and roots, sometimes cooked them, sometimes used them as poultices. Many of these leaves and roots are used in modern medicines.

The use of honey as a "medicine" is probably older than the history of medicine. Primitive man couldn't possibly have avoided experimenting with honey for his ailments. Because this was the nature of primitive man—to experiment. He had no one to consult. He looked to nature for his survival, and to his own resources.

Honey was available. It was at hand. The first person who smeared a cut or bruise with honey and found that it helped, must have passed his remarkable cure on to someone else.

References to honey as a popular medicine, even as a magic healer, are found in the Bible, the Talmud, the Koran, and other religious tracts. In ancient China honey was utilized as a medicine; the same was true in ancient India, Persia, Arabia, Assyria, Greece.

Hippocrates, the "father of medicine," was a great believer in the therapeutic attributes of honey. According to him the physical virtues of honey were as follows: "It causes heat, cleans sores and ulcers, softens hard ulcers of the lips, heals carbuncles and running sores." He recommended honey for difficulty in breathing.

The ancients believed that people who ate quantities of honey became more congenial and affectionate. Honey was considered a cure for bitter feelings or an unpleasant disposition. In the folklore of almost all nations the magic and curative powers of honey are extolled.

The Talmud recommended the use of honey for ulcerated wounds, in humans and animals alike. During the Middle Ages honey, plain or mixed with other ingredients, was used in treating boils, wounds, burns and ulcers. One particular remedy was made by boiling honey, vinegar and winter-green, to be applied like a poultice or a plaster. Rectal suppositories contained honey and wax. For enemas honey and oil was a popular treatment.

Among the country folk of central and eastern Europe certain "honey ointments" were used extensively for all kinds of wounds. One such ointment was made of a mixture of honey and flour. Another was made of honey and burnt alum. Drops of warm honey were used for earaches and also, not necessarily heated, for inflamed and infected eyes. In one instance a farmer used honey drops to cure the eyes of his horse. According to the story, the horse was going blind; his eyes were covered with a white film and they watered profusely. He seemed to be suffering great pain. The farmer dipped white honey into the eyes of the horse with a feather for several nights and the irritation disappeared. Even today in some parts of the world honey in the form of eyedrops is used for treating trachoma.

The Germans believed strongly in the curative power of honey and used it both internally and externally. They made an ointment of cod liver oil and honey which they used for dressing wounds.

The early settlers in America brought with them from the "old country" many of their folk cures. In the New England states, particularly, folk medicine is still very popular. Farmers of today have many problems their forbears didn't have. Pollution, of the air, of the earth, destruction of the balance of nature by bull-dozing, highways and super-structures, all combine to compound the ordinary "natural" problems farmers encounter.

New problems create new tensions, but many of the folk treatments come from old sources. Honey and apple cider vinegar are two old-fashioned hardy favorites of practitioners of folk medicine in New England.

For headaches they recommend inhalation of fumes from apple cider vinegar. Equal parts of the vinegar and water are heated in a basin, then the person is advised to lean over the basin and inhale "fifty to seventy times." If the headache disappears and later returns, it's recommended that the treatment be repeated.

Honey is also recommended in the curing of headaches, especially migraine headaches. The suggested folk remedy is to take a full tablespoon of honey immediately upon the onset of a migraine, and follow it with another tablespoonful if the first one doesn't work.

A friend of the author who suffers from migraine headaches decided to test out the remedy. She took a brimming tablespoonful of honey as soon as she felt the twinges of a migraine coming on. The headache subsided, but returned in about an hour. She took another tablespoonful of honey, then sat in a tub of warm water for about half an hour. Her headache disappeared and she went to bed. She awakened sometime in the night with another headache. At this point she "figured out" that her body must need water. She arose, drank three glasses of water and her headache disappeared completely and didn't recur!

Her reasoning as to why the honey helped her runs like this: Migraine headaches come from tension. Honey is a "relaxer." If by taking the honey she relaxed her tensions, her body automatically cured the headache. As to the water, she claims that was just a hunch, having to do with the whole idea that honey absorbs moisture and that therefore her body required additional liquid. She reported her cure to her physician and he said that in order to accept her treatments as valid a series of tests would have to be conducted with different people, some using honey, some not, over a period of time. "It would difficult.... But," he added, "if it works for you, *great* ... by all means use it ... it beats pills!"

Doctors are reluctant to accept folk cures without substantiated proof, which would require scientifically controlled tests and studies. One basis for their feeling is the danger of self-diagnosis and self-treatment. Yet often doctors resort to folk cures after they've ascertained that a patient isn't suffering from some serious organic or functional disorder which requires more sophisticated treatment than a teaspoonful of honey.

While doctors tend to be skeptical of home remedies their patients are quick to point out the many mistakes doctors have made both in diagnosis and treatment. Doctors themselves often admit to mistakes.

One retired physician sadly recounted to the author how many of his patients suffered serious kidney disorder as a result of being treated with sulfanilamide some years ago. Yet the same sulfanilamide cured the condition for which he prescribed it and was a recognized and accepted form of treatment.

The same story may be told about other medications, which, upon being introduced to the medical profession, are hailed as "wonder drugs." In the early days of penicillin doctors prescribed it freely. It was and still is a remarkably effective medication. Yet many people experienced violent reactions, even death, as a result of being treated with penicillin. Similar reactions occur with other medications. There are people who have a sensitivity or an allergy to certain medical drugs or antibiotics—

something they don't know until after they suffer serious after-effects as a result of using one.

Most medication carries on it some explanation of what possible side effects might occur. Physicians take these side effects into consideration when they prescribe, sometimes warning the patient, sometimes not. Often they feel the good the medication does will offset any possible harm.

One young doctor internist told the author: "It's a touchy thing. If you tell a patient he may experience dizziness, nausea, or whatever, if he takes a certain medication, he may very well imagine these things happening to him. And if you don't tell him and something happens, then, of course, he blames the doctor. I always instruct the patients to call me back and let me know how they're feeling . . . but few do."

In all the tales about honey cures no mention has ever been made of anyone being allergic or sensitive to honey, or of having suffered any serious consequences as a result of using honey internally or externally.

Several people interviewed by the author mentioned using honey for bad skin burns, and all reported how the pain disappeared and burns healed soon after the application of honey. Some told of using honey on cuts. The author cut her finger while opening a can of honey. She immediately applied a smear of honey and covered the cut with a band-aid. The pain disappeared almost immediately and the cut healed, without the usual swelling and skin discoloration associated with deep under-the-skin cuts, by the following day. She changed the "honey dressing" three times.

The external application of honey is at least as old as history. The ancient Egyptians used it as a surgical dressing. They also believed honey helped relieve inflammation of the eyelids and the eyes. The Hindus and the Chinese are said to have used honey as an ointment on small-pox patients. They believed it prevented scars and quickened the healing of the pustules.

Up to the end of the nineteenth century honey enjoyed a reputation as a therapeutic substance. With the advent of packaged patented, well-advertised medications, its popularity waned. Only among country folk and backwoods people has it retained its importance as a remedy for certain ailments of men and domestic animals.

Folk medicine is still popular in rural areas of Vermont. It is used particularly for treating hay fever, which is common to the region. One of the treatments is to locate the pollen causing the hay fever and feed the victim honey made from that pollen. Also, hay fever victims are instructed to chew on honeycombs before the onset of and during the hay fever season, and to take honey mixed with apple cider vinegar three or four times a day. Chewing of the honeycomb is supposed to keep the nasal passages open, and the honey acts as a relaxer. The effectiveness of the treatment and its results depend on the severity of the condition. In mild and moderate cases, the hay fever has been checked and in severe cases the individual gains some degree of comfort.

Many reasons have been given as to why honey acts the way it does in the human system. Primarily it may be said that the same attributes of honey which make it a healthy natural food make it therapeutically effective. To separate the dietetic and medical values of honey is virtually impossible.

Nutritionists know that wholesome, healthy natural food preserves health and prevents illness. Honey is such a food. Besides, honey is a natural source of energy. When a person suffers from some chronic ailment which causes him to feel tired or run-down a spoonful of honey taken regularly several times a day is bound to make him feel better. Also, honey, because it acts as a soporific, relieves tension caused by illness or fatigue. It's not accidental that even doctors tell their high-strung patients to "drink a cup of hot tea with a teaspoonful of honey" before retiring, as a means of helping them fall asleep; or, that they often prescribe hot tea, lemon juice and honey for the common cold.

The sugars in honey are quickly assimilated by the body; they do not tax the digestive system. When a person is ill the consumption of honey places less strain on the body and helps the body fight disease germs.

Honey is used in cough syrups and cough drops. An old-fashioned remedy for coughs is made with lemon juice, honey and glycerine. Eucalyptus honey is considered excellent in the treatment of sore throats.

Eucalyptus honey has a history all its own. It seems the cultivation of eucalyptus trees in regions infested with malaria helped eradicate that disease. In certain regions of Australia malaria is said to have completely disappeared after fast-growing eucalyptus trees were planted.

Another story is told about a Trappist monastery near Rome which was built by monks many years ago on malaria-infested soil. After the monks planted eucalyptus trees malaria disappeared. At the same time the monks built extensive apiaries for the bees and harvested eucalyptus honey which they sold on the European market for its medicinal value.

It's claimed that eucalyptus honey is strengthening, blood-forming, blood-purifying, nourishing, and appetite-producing. Australia is one of the larger producers of eucalyptus honey.

Stories of honey cures come from unusual sources. In a recent issue of the *American Bee Journal* the following letter appeared:

> My daughter . . . bought a puppy dog to be a pet for her 3-year-old son. The dog became sick and was taken to a veterinarian who fed it medicine for worms. The medicine caused the dog to become very sick and refuse to eat. He was again taken to the vet who said that there was nothing that he could do for it, but that the pup might be fed some molasses or honey which might cause it to begin feeding again. . . . [She] gave it some molasses which it promptly threw up. She waited about two hours, then fed it some honey which stayed down and caused the dog to begin eating again. It is now O.K.

Primitive, ancient, medieval, and modern man seem to have used honey for similar ailments: as a treatment for cuts and burns, as a remedy for gastric and intestinal disorders, in treating respiratory disorders, as a salve for skin diseases and in surgical dressings, for inflammation of the eyes and eyelids, as a tranquilizer.

Some day the medical profession may make exhaustive tests to prove scientifically the virtues of honey as a healer. Meanwhile, people will probably go on using it because it makes them feel good and because "it works."

10

HONEY IN SYMBOLISM, POETRY AND PROVERBS

Honey, a symbol of purity, wisdom, beauty, in religion, took on similar characteristics in poetry and song. To many writers it has represented all things sweet and pleasing to the tongue, to the heart and to the mind. Even today in popular songs and current expressions the term "honey" appears often.

The beehive has shared with honey the attention of poets and lyricists from many lands.

The Greeks and Romans called the bees "the birds of the muses." To sweeten the verses of the poets, golden bees were said to have gathered honey from the thyme that covered Mount Hymettus.

Like ancient Hindu wedding ceremonies, ancient Hindu poetry was literally "drenched" in honey. The Sanskrit word *madhukara* (honeyborn) had three meanings: *bee*, *lover* and *moon*. Love-mak-

ing and honey seemed to go together, as typified in
the following excerpt from the Rig-Veda (early
Hindu religious book):

My tongue has honey at the tip, and sweetest
     honey at the root
Thou yieldest to my wish and will and shall
     be mine and only mine
My coming in is honey sweet and honey sweet
     my going forth
My voice and words are sweet
I fain would be like honey in my look
Around thee have I girt a zone of sugar-cane
     to banish hate
That thou may'st be in love with me my dar-
     ling never to depart.

In India the entire aura surrounding the sex act
is one of beauty. The senses play an important role
in descriptive phrases about women. Old Hindu
writings went into expressive detail on the subject
of feminine charms.

In one book women are classified according to
their sex scent. "The Lotus-woman is fair, soft and
plump, her sex organs resemble a lotus and are
scented like a lily. The Art-woman is slim, co-
quettish, not highly sexed, and her sex organs have
the scent of honey. The Conch-woman is large,
rather hairy, and passionate. Her organs have a
salty scent. And, finally, the Elephant-woman, who
is short, broad, large-hipped and walks with a slow
slouching walk. Her characteristic smell is like that
of an elephant and she takes a long time to attain
sexual satisfaction."

Yoga, which originated in India six thousand
years ago, also emphasizes the beauty of sex.
Among non-ascetic Yogis love-making is consid-

ered an art to be indulged in leisurely, almost like
a ceremony.

Because honey induces a feeling of sensuous
well-being, it blends naturally into the voluptuous
texture of Hindu love-making. As one imaginative
writer said: "Honey—golden, amber—vibrates with
the very color of orgasm."

From Hindu mythology comes another poetic
description of woman, this having to do with her
creation. According to the myth of Hindu Vulcan,
Twasktrie, mixed a little honey in with other materials. The ingredients were "the buoyancy of the
leaves, the velvety gloss of the fawn, the brilliancy
of the sun's rays, the tears of the mist, the incon-
stancy of the winds, the trepidation of the hare,
the vanity of the peacock, the softness of the dawn
on the throat of the swallow, the hardness of the
diamond, the sweetness of honey, the cruelty of
the tiger, the warmth of fire, the chill of snow, the
chatter of the jay, and the cooing of the dove." He
put them all together and presented Woman to
Man.

Many poems glorify the bees, not only for their
exemplary life, but for providing mankind with
honey. Two contrasting examples, written by Englishmen, follow; the first by Sir Isaac Watts, who
lived in the eighteenth century, and the second by
William Shakespeare, who lived in the sixteenth
and early seventeenth centuries.

How doth the little busy bee
Improve each shining hour
And gather honey all the day
From every opening flower!

How skilfully she builds her cell!
How neat she spreads the wax

And labors hard to store it well
With the sweet food she makes.
        —Sir Isaac Watts, from *Against Idleness and
Mischief*

For so work the honey bees
Creatures that by a rule in nature teach
The act of order to a peopled kingdom
They have a king and officers of sorts
Where some, like magistrates, correct at home,
Others, like merchants, venture trade abroad.
Others, like soldiers, armed in their stings,
Make boot upon the summer's velvet buds;
Which pillage they with merry march bring
    home
To the tent-royal of their emperor;
Who busied in his majesty, surveys
The singing masons building roofs of gold,
The civil citizens kneading up the honey,
The poor mechanic porters crowding in
Their heavy burdens at his narrow gate,
The sad-eyed justice, with his surly hum,
Delivering o'er to executors pale
The lazy yawning drone.
            —William Shakespeare from *Henry V*

A charming poem that mentions honey was written
by Edward Lear, who lived in the nineteenth century. According to the first stanza:

The Owl and the Pussy Cat went to sea
In a beautiful pea-green boat.
They took some honey, and plenty of money
Wrapped up in a five-pound note.
The Owl looked up to the stars above
And sang to a small guitar

chyt, 10

'O lovely Pussy! O Pussy, my love
What a beautiful Pussy you are!'

In American folklore and folksongs the term
"honey" is used as a term of endearment. In the
South children (and adults) are called "honey-
chile" to express affection. Often "honey" has sexual
connotations, as in the expression "taste of honey"
or "dip your wick in honey." But always the context is one of pleasure.

Proverbs make frequent use of the word "honey."
Some of the more popular are:

*A drop of honey catches more flies than a barrel
of vinegar.*

*Feed a man vinegar and you'll eat no honey
from his lips.*

*If you want to gather honey, don't kick over the
beehive.* (Abraham Lincoln)

Honey young, wine old.

No bees, no honey; no work, no money.

Who is afraid of the sting never earns honey.

chpt. 11
questions 97 to 100

11

USES OF HONEY

Honey has traveled through history alongside man and has been used by man in many ways: as a sweetener, a food, a healer, a symbol, an aphrodisiac, a drink, a medium of exchange, a measure of wealth, health, beauty, wisdom, eloquence.

Some uses for honey border on the bizarre. For some unknown reason honey seems to draw people to it. One ingenious student, interviewed by the author, explained honey's attraction in a unique sophistic syllogism: "Honey attracts moisture. People are about 90 percent water. Therefore, honey attracts people."

Of all the uses for honey, one of the most original was described in a recent issue of the *Australian Beekeeper*. Honey was used by burglars in an Australian house-breaking. A window at the house had been smashed, after first sticking on it a paper soaked in honey. Reason for the honey: to muffle the sound of breaking glass!

Another story concerns a European spy who posed as a beekeeper. In one hive he kept a transmitter, in another a radio receiver. Meanwhile, bees buzzing around his cottage kept police away. (The story doesn't mention what he did with the honeycombs, or what the bees did about the radio equipment.)

A recent article in the *American Bee Journal* states that the American Honey Institute is conducting a survey to learn from the consumer how, when, and where he uses honey, and why. The author conducted her own survey, and here are some of the more colorful results:

From a former opera singer:

"Honey? The only way I take honey is in booze! You want to know something? The best way to cure a cold ... a tablespoon of honey and a jigger of whiskey! That'll do it! Take it before you go to bed and ... you wake up cured!"   She laughed. "And you want to know something else? Before Caruso sang an aria he took some honey, lemon juice and whiskey. Said it opened his throat.... And it does, believe me! I've tried it myself!"

From a twenty-eight-year-old legal secretary, born and raised in England:

"Back home, we eat lots of honey. On biscuits, scones, crumpets ... but you Americans have some clever ideas about honey ... I'm married to one, and ..."—she blushed—"every night before he retires he drinks a mixture of honey, raw egg, milk and a drop or two of sherry.... He claims it makes him virile!"

From a four-year-old pre-schooler:

"Gee, I think it grows on bushes, or in flowers ...

or maybe it comes from cows.... I sure like Winnie the Pooh and the honey tree!"

Honey seems to be a kind of family affair. Invariably, a mother, grandmother, an aunt, a grandfather, someone of another generation, is involved. Honey recipes and remedies are passed from person to person.

Today, honey is used primarily as a food. It's eaten out of the spoon, on bread and fruits, in tea, coffee, fruit drinks, milk, ice cream, cereals. It's used extensively in commercial baking. Honey is used for curing meats. One honey distributor told the author he "sells lots of honey to race horse owners who put it into the food."

Honey not sold to the consumer market is sold to firms who make animal food.

The wife of a honey distributor told about an experience she had with honey:

My husband's been in the honey business, one way or the other, for fifteen years ... and I've heard lots of stories about how honey's good for this and good for that.... But I'm kinda skeptical about what I hear.... But, listen to this! Not long ago my mother came back from a trip to Mexico with a bad case of Montezuma's Revenge. It was a weekend, I couldn't get a doctor and she was really bad off ... must've lost about ten pounds in two days. She had the runs bad. My husband wasn't home and I didn't know what to do. I was really worried. So, I gave her a spoonful of sage honey. She began feeling better.... I gave her more and the next day she was fine! When my husband came home he said 'sage honey was the best thing' I could've given her!

At a recent "powder puff" derby of pre-teen girls playing football, the athletic director showed up with a large jar of honey and box full of plastic spoons. He handed each girl a spoon and said: "Eat a spoonful of honey before you go out on the field . . . and in between quarters I'll be here with the honey jar if any of you need an extra zoom of energy!"

Part II

COOKING WITH HONEY

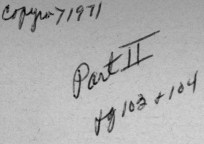

1

MAGICAL, MYSTICAL COOKERY
WITH HONEY

Almost from the beginning of civilization, honey foods have radiated a certain specialness. Among primitive peoples they were used in offerings to the gods. Even the sophisticated Greeks used honey cakes in their religious ceremonies, as did the Egyptians and the Romans.

Christians, Jews, and Moslems, wherever they dwelt, had special holiday foods made with honey. Some of the important honey holidays coincided with the spring honey harvest. The Jewish holiday of Passover and the Christian Easter, both in the spring, are said by some historians to have originated as agricultural holidays. Each of these holidays calls for special honey treats.

Immigrants to the United States brought their "old country" honey recipes and cooked them for special feast days. Many of these recipes passed from generation to generation by word of mouth. Some were recorded, some lost.

Today, second- and third-generation Americans are creating new imaginative honey foods and adopting or adapting many of the old country recipes to their modern cuisines.

Cooking with honey is cooking with a touch of magic! Honey gives to everything a special bouquet that cannot be described—it's something almost mysterious, *felt* rather than tasted.

Honey blends well, it's water-soluble, it never gets lumpy or curdy. Its satiny texture enhances cake and cookie batters, as well as sauces and puddings. As a glaze it is superb. One caution must be observed in using honey: Be careful not to over-honey foods, unless you want the taste of honey to predominate. Honey used in proper proportion lends a special character to food; it doesn't "take over."

Cooking with honey may be compared to cooking with herbs. It requires subtlety to be most effective. In fine cooking, the herbs must never be actually *tasted;* they, too, should be *felt*. The same holds true with spices. No spice should predominate, unless it's intended to, as in gingerbread or ginger cookies.

Honey's definite flavor when eaten alone becomes diffused when blended with vegetables, fruits, meats, poultry, cereals, and other foodstuffs.

In cooking and baking, only the mild-flavored honeys such as clover and alfalfa should be used—unless a predominating flavor is desired. For example, in making an orange-flavored glaze for chicken or duck an orange-blossom honey might be used. Mild blended honeys are excellent for cooking and baking.

2

HELPFUL HINTS FOR COOKING AND BAKING

MEASURING HONEY

Wet the measuring cup or spoon and the honey will easily slide off. Whenever possible, use the utensil in which the oil was measured for the honey as well.

Level off the top with a spatula. Honey tends to overfill or "round out" in a spoon or cup before it drips over. Also scrape honey residue from the sides and bottom with a scraper. (Whatever can't be scraped off is good for licking.)

It's a good idea to store honey in a container with a cut-off lid, like the kind used for pancake syrups. In that way you can stop the flow of honey easily. Also, learn to stop pouring before the honey has reached the top of the measuring utensil. The last few drips will generally fill the required amount.

MIXING THE HONEY

Honey blends well with cooking and baking ingredients. Some recipes call for mixing honey with the liquid, others call for mixing honey with eggs or with oil. It's best to pour the honey slowly in a steady stream into whatever it's being mixed with, stirring or mixing as it flows.

If honey is mixed with something cold it will thicken slightly, but eventually it will loosen up as the temperature of the whole mixture increases. As in all recipes it's best to mix honey with ingredients such as eggs, milk, cheese, butter or margarine, at room temperature.

SUBSTITUTING HONEY FOR SUGAR
(IN BAKING)

The sweetness of honey varies according to the proportion of fruit sugar it contains, and fruit sugar content varies in different types of honey. However, because of the water content in honey it averages about the same sweetness, measure for measure, as ordinary sugar; that is to say, a cup of sugar and a cup of honey would have the same sweetness level.

Since the average moisture content in most honeys runs around 18 percent, some cooking authorities recommend reducing the amount of liquid in a recipe by *one-quarter cup for each cup of honey used*. This is a safe procedure to follow. In other words, if a recipe calls for one cup of sugar and one cup of milk you would use one cup of honey and ¾ cup of milk. (The author, who likes less sweetening than most recipes provide, reduces the amount of honey by one-quarter when substituting for sugar and uses the called-for amount of liquid.)

Some degree of experimentation is often required in making substitutions, since moisture content of honeys varies. Tupelo, sage, orange-blossom, buckwheat, to name a few, have a higher than average moisture content. These varieties are best served as spreads, on crackers, bread, pancakes or biscuits to fully appreciate the special quality of their flavors.

Foods made with honey brown faster than those made with sugar, because the fruit sugar contained in honey caramelizes when subjected to a high temperature.

Always reduce the called-for temperature by 25 degrees when substituting honey for sugar. For example, if the recipe calls for baking at 375°F., bake at 350°F. when using honey.

GENERAL

Honey-sweetened baked goods are more flavorful the next day.

Honey cakes and cookies are tender and moist. They also absorb moisture and flavors from other foods and from the atmosphere. They should be stored separately or wrapped in moisture-proof paper such as waxed paper, tinfoil, or plastic.

HOW TO FREEZE BAKED GOODS MADE WITH HONEY

Bread and rolls: Cool thoroughly. Wrap in freezer paper and freeze. When ready to use remove from freezer and allow to thaw in wrapper. Place in slow oven (300°F.) for twenty to thirty minutes.

Cakes: For best results freeze without frosting and wrap each layer separately in freezing paper or foil. When ready to use, allow to thaw in package for about ten minutes, then place in slow oven for 10 minutes (300°F.). May also be thawed in wrapper at room temperature for about three hours.

Frosted Cakes: Freeze without wrapping. When solidly frozen, wrap in foil or freezing paper. Allow to unthaw in the wrapper. Butter cream and uncooked frostings are best for freezing.

Cookies: Pack in cardboard boxes between layers of heavy wax paper or aluminum foil. Thaw at room temperature.

Unbaked Cookie Rolls: Wrap in heavy wax paper and freeze. When ready to bake thaw at room temperature just enough to slice. Bake as any other cookie dough made with honey.

Unbaked Drop Cookies: Freeze on cookie sheet. When solidly frozen, pack in cardboard boxes between layers of heavy wax paper or aluminum foil. When ready to use, place on cookie sheet, allow to thaw at room temperature, and bake as freshly made product.

3

JELLIES, JAMS, AND PRESERVES MADE WITH HONEY

Honey may be substituted for half the sugar in making jellies, jams and preserves. More honey than this is likely to mask the delicate flavor of the fruit and change the color and consistency of the product.

In making jelly with honey, use only strong-flavored juices, high in pectin and acid. Since honey causes foaming, watch the juice during cooking, or, better yet, cook slightly beyond the usual jelly test.

A jelly with a pronounced honey flavor may be made in the following proportions:

> 1 cup honey
> ¼ cup water
> ⅜ cup of liquid fruit pectin

Heat the honey and water to boiling, stirring constantly. Add the liquid fruit pectin and heat just to boiling. This jelly has a very delicate texture.

Perfect jam or jelly with all honey requires the use of commercial fruit pectin. Follow directions, step-by-step, as given on the label of the pectin. Use exactly the same amount of honey as other sweeteners.

4

HONEY SYRUPS FOR CANNING AND FREEZING FRUITS

CANNING

A syrup may be made by first boiling the water, then removing the water from the heat and adding honey.

The proportion of honey to water should be: one cup honey to four cups water—for a light syrup; 1½ cups honey to four cups water—for a medium syrup.

This should be sufficient for six quart-size containers or jars.

The syrup may be stored in the refrigerator and will be ready for use when needed.

FREEZING

Fruit may be frozen in the same syrup as used for canning.

The advantage to using honey, aside from its health-giving attributes, is the fact that fruits frozen in all-honey syrup do not require the use of Vitamin C powder, tablets or ascorbic acid to prevent browning or darkening of the fruit.

The amount of honey may be varied, according to taste.

5

HONEY IN DRINKS

In ancient and medieval times, among royalty and peasants alike, the consumption of alcoholic and non-alcoholic beverages was more prevalent than today, because drinking water wasn't always easily attainable—or very good to drink when it was available. Most of these beverages were made with honey; grapes for wine didn't come into common usage in Europe until around the middle of the eighteenth century—about the same time honey began to wane in popularity.

The most common and famous of all honey "brews" was mead, which is referred to in Old English as meth, in early Greek writings as hydromel. Each country seems to have had its own special method for brewing the mead, but the basic ingredients of all meads were honey and water. Proportions varied as did cooking time and period for fermentation.

Among some groups the making of mead was treated with such reverence that before its preparation the priests consulted the stars to select the best time for concocting the mead. In some instances the reverence for mead went to such extremes as to forbid sexual intercourse during the period of fermentation, lest the mead spoil.

Embellishments such as thyme, ginger, nutmeg, cinnamon, cloves, pepper, sesame flour, sweet marjoram, rosemary, even whites of eggs, have been added to enhance the flavor of the mead.

During the Middle Ages mead was frequently made from crushed honeycombs, which were steeped in water, strained and then put into earthen vessels until the liquid fermented. Wooden kegs were considered preferable for storing mead, and it was believed the longer the mead aged the mellower its flavor.

History is full of stories about mead drinking. The Anglo-Saxons and Vikings were notorious for the amount of mead they consumed. Before they went into battle they drank huge quantities of mead and afterward victories were celebrated with more drinking bouts.

Mead sometimes came in for some odd usage, other than drinking. In one incident in medieval Germany, in the early eleventh century, hostile tribes tried to burn the town of Meissen. Because there was a shortage of water, the inhabitants extinguished the flames with their reserve stock of mead!

The Russians have a drink they call *miod*, also made with honey, of the same strength as beer.

Among the French, mead drinking was discouraged because of their wine industry. But it's believed that some meads were bottled and sold as wines and that among the peasants meads were as freely drunk as elsewhere.

Essentially, the beginning of any mead is honey and water. To this may be added varieties of fruit juices, lemon rind, cinnamon sticks, raisins, depending on the creativity and imagination of the maker. The mixture doesn't have to be cooked, and may be stored in an open vessel (covered with a towel) at room temperature. Mead is not allowed to ferment. Among Moslems, who are forbidden alcoholic beverages, simple mead is commonly drunk.

The recipe for making simple mead is as follows:
Mix one part honey and three parts water.
Boil slowly over a low flame until about one-third of the original amount has evaporated.
Skim the surface and pour into a cask. Place in a cool place. It's ready for drinking in three or four days.
(*Note:* The amount of honey may be increased or decreased according to taste.)

As in the making of an exquisite French sauce, mead should be tasted as it's being mixed. If it's too sweet, add more lemon; if too tart, more honey. Apple juice goes well in mead. A good mead base may be made from *one part honey, one part apple juice, two parts water*. From this beginning the adventurous mead-maker is on his own!

The fermentation period may be anywhere up to thirty days. But just as the ancients argued about the proper length of time for fermentation, modern mead-makers differ. A little activated yeast may be added to speed up the fermentation, although honey on its own, mixed with water, sitting at room temperature, should ferment without help.

The wife of a Los Angeles honey distributor obtained for the author a recipe for mead from one of her customers—a young man who makes it regularly. He told her he obtained the recipe from his grandmother, who came from England. At the time, he was searching for a "proper" wine cask, but, meanwhile was using a large glass jug for his honey brew.

Here's the recipe:

"My Grandmother's Mead"

1 gallon water
4 pounds honey
6 cloves
2 sticks cinnamon
Juice and peel of two lemons

Boil combined ingredients slowly for thirty minutes.

Strain into an earthenware crock, leaving plenty of room for expansion.

After the mixture cools, add a teaspoonful of activated yeast for each gallon of liquid.

Store in a cool place (about 55 degrees) for at least a month. The crock should be covered with a towel.

Mead-making at home is fun, and invites all sorts of improvisations! And, to add to the fun, as the mead-makers of old used to do, stir from time to time with a long wooden ladle—and lick the ladle!

In some of the old-time recipes for mead the

cask is allowed to stay open in a warm room and is stirred from time to time. Some recipes also call for the addition of whiskey, brandy, or gin to strengthen the flavor. Others call for cherries, strawberries, gooseberries. Many variations may be obtained by using different types of honey and varying the proportions of honey to water.

After the mead has fermented to taste, bottle and refrigerate. Some mead connoisseurs say it should be served at room temperature, or "Just slightly chilled."

Part II
Chpt. 6
gres from pg. 119 to 122..

6

OTHER HONEY DRINKS

Honey blends well with fruit juices, milk, and alcoholic beverages. It may be substituted for sugar in any drink where sugar is called for. Less honey should be used than sugar to avoid a "honeyed" taste—unless that taste is desired. The best method to follow when substituting honey is to start with less, then add more if necessary.

If honey rather than sugar is used for sweetening lemonade or lime juice, the result is a much more healthful drink, since the honey is more easily assimilated by the body and gives stored energy.

The following recipes are but a small sampling of the many drinks that may be prepared with honey. For those who like to improvise, the recipes may inspire other concoctions!

Fruit Punch

1 cup honey
1 cup orange juice (fresh)
½ cup lemon juice (fresh)
1 cup crushed fresh fruit in season
1½ cups freshly made, strong tea
⅛ teaspoon salt
1 pint ginger ale

In a large punch bowl mix all the ingredients except the ginger ale. Just before serving add chopped ice and ginger ale. If the punch is strong, dilute with ice water or more ginger ale.)

For a pickup with staying powers, here is a quick-energy drink—or a "breakfast in a glass."

"Pepper-Up" Cocktail

1 egg, separated
1 tablespoon honey
Juice of one orange
Juice of half a lemon

Beat egg yolk, honey, and fruit juices with rotor beater until fluffy. Beat egg white separately and fold into the first mixture.

For special occasions this cocktail may be served in sherbet glasses and topped with a cherry or sprinkled with chopped mint.

Honey may be used in preparing hot chocolate,

the amount depending on the degree of sweetness desired. Here is a sample recipe:

Honeyed Chocolate

2 tablespoons cocoa
½ teaspoon salt
3 tablespoons honey
2 cups scalded milk

Blend cocoa, salt, and honey. Add to the scalded milk and simmer for about five minutes. (This may be served cold by pouring over chipped ice.)

For people who have no time to fix breakfast, here's a delicious and very sturdy "breakfast in a glass"—healthy, beautiful, and nourishing!

Fruit-Honey Vitality Drink

¼ cup honey
½ cup unsweetened pineapple juice
1 mashed banana
1 egg
1 cup milk

Put all the ingredients into a blender and mix until frothy. The ingredients may also be blended with a whisk or rotor beater.)

For an added "touch of madness" splash a speck of cognac or sherry into the mixture and drink for a midnight snack. People who've tried it say it makes for good sleeping. (Some claim it has aphrodisiac effects.)

Mead-making is becoming popular among young people. It's part of the whole new life pattern of self-expression and creativity evidenced by a revived interest in the home arts, such as crewel embroidery, knitting, macrame and crocheting.

In metropolitan areas throughout the country there are specialty shops devoted to the "wine-making arts," where necessary crocks and other equipment may be obtained for making wines. The author interviewed one of the proprietors of such a shop, and he told her he had "about fifty or sixty recipes just for making mead."

Approx 7, 1971

Part II
chpt. 7
goes from pg. 123 to 130

7

BREADS, CAKES, COOKIES, MUFFINS

Numerous recipes are available for breads, cakes, cookies and muffins prepared with honey. Almost everyone the author interviewed had a "special" honey recipe. The California Honey Advisory Board provides honey recipes, as does the Department of Agriculture.

Those presented here were kitchen- and taste-tested by the author.

As mentioned earlier, bakery goods made with honey retain their freshness longer than those baked with other sweetening agents. They also have a slightly different texture: more body, more substance.

① Cranberry Nut Bread

Combine the following ingredients:

> *3 cups biscuit mix*
> *¼ teaspoon salt*
> *½ teaspoon cinnamon*
> *1 cup fresh cranberries coarsely chopped*
> *1 cup chopped walnuts*

Combine the following in another bowl:

> *1 slightly beaten egg*
> *1 cup honey*
> *½ cup milk*

Add the second mixture to the first, stirring only until the flour is thoroughly dampened. The batter will be thick.

Pour into a well-oiled loaf pan, 9 x 9 x 3 inches.

Bake in preheated 350°F. oven (moderate) 45-50 minutes, or until a toothpick inserted in center comes out clean.

Delicious *as is*, or toasted and served with cream cheese!

② Golden Orange Loaf

Sift together the following:

> *2½ cups presifted unbleached white flour*
> *1 tablespoon baking powder*
> *1 teaspoon salt*

Combine the following in another bowl and beat until smooth:

>   3 eggs
>   ½ cup honey
>   2 tablespoons soft butter or margarine

Add to the egg mixture:

>   1 cup orange marmalade

Gradually add the sifted dry ingredients to the egg-honey-marmalade mixture, stirring well after each addition. The batter will be fairly thick.

Spoon the batter into a greased 9 x 5 x 3 inch loaf pan.

Bake in preheated oven at 350°F. for 50-60 minutes or until done. (Test with toothpick in center of loaf.) After removing from oven cool in pan for 5 minutes. Remove from pan and place on wire rack.

② Honey Date Loaf Cake

>   2 tablespoons shortening
>   ½ cup honey
>   1 egg
>   1 teaspoon grated lemon rind
>   2 teaspoons lemon juice
>   1½ cups sifted unbleached white flour
>   ⅛ teaspoon salt
>   ⅜ teaspoon baking soda
>   1 teaspoon baking powder
>   ½ cup sour milk or buttermilk

   1 cup chopped dates
   ½ cup chopped walnuts or sunflower seeds

Cream shortening. Gradually beat in honey. Add egg, lemon rind and juice. Beat thoroughly.

Sift dry ingredients, and add alternately with sour milk, to egg mixture.

Add dates and nuts.

Pour into greased loaf pan (9 x 4 inches). Bake in preheated oven at 350°F. for 50-60 minutes or until a skewer inserted in center comes out clean.

NOTE: This cake is moist inside.

(#) Honey Prune Loaf

Sift together the following dry ingredients:

   2 cups unbleached white flour (sifted
      before measuring)
   3 teaspoons baking powder
   ½ teaspoon baking soda
   1 teaspoon salt

Add to the sifted ingredients:

   1 cup quick cooking oatmeal

Beat together in another bowl:

   2 eggs
   ¼ cup salad oil
   ¾ cup milk
   ¾ cup honey

Add this mixture to the dry ingredients. Fold in

1 cup chopped pitted prunes, uncooked. The batter will be thick.

Spoon into greased 9 x 5 x 3 inch loaf pan. Bake in preheated oven at 350°F. for about 1 hour, or until done when tested in center.

Cool in pan for five minutes. Remove from pan and continue cooling on wire rack.

⑤ Honey Apple Puffs

Sift together the following:

> *2 cups presifted unbleached white flour*
> *3 teaspoons baking powder*
> *1 teaspoon salt*
> *½ teaspoon cinnamon*
> *¼ teaspoon nutmeg*

Add the following ingredients:

> *1 cup whole wheat or bran cereal flakes*
> *¼ cup finely chopped walnuts*
> *½ cup raisins*
> *1 cup shredded pared apple.*

Combine in separate bowl:

> *2 well beaten eggs*
> *⅔ cup honey*
> *½ cup milk*
> *¼ cup salad oil*

Add the liquid mixture all at once to the flour mixture, stirring just enough to blend. The batter should be lumpy.

Spoon into greased muffin tins (or foil lined muffin cups). Fill about ⅔rds. full. Makes 18 muffins.

Bake in preheated 400°F. oven for 18-20 minutes, or until golden brown. Serve warm with honey butter.

Ⓛ Date Bars

> 1½ cups sifted flour
> 1 teaspoon baking powder
> ½ teaspoon salt
> 3 eggs
> 1 cup honey
> 1 teaspoon vanilla
> 1¾ cups chopped dates
> 1 cup chopped nuts
> ½ cup halved candied cherries (optional)

Re-sift flour with baking powder and salt. Beat eggs until very frothy in a large mixing bowl. Gradually beat in honey, adding it in a fine stream. Add vanilla. Stir in flour and dates, nuts and cherries. Mix well.

Spread on greased 9 x 13½-inch pan. Bake at 350°F. 35-45 minutes. Cool thoroughly. Cut into bars. Store tightly covered or freeze. Yield: 30 bars.

① Chinese Crispies

> 1 cup honey
> 1 cup chunk-style peanut butter
> ¼ cup undiluted evaporated milk
> 1 teaspoon vanilla

1 tablespoon unbleached white flour
1 3-oz. can chow mein noodles

Mix together all ingredients except noodles. Then, fold in noodles. Chill 30 minutes in refrigerator. Drop by teaspoonfuls on greased cookie sheet.

Bake at 300°F. (slow) 20 minutes. Remove from cookie sheet and cook on rack. Makes three dozen cookies.

⑧ Honey Soya Cookies

¼ cup butter or margarine
⅜ cup natural brown sugar
1 egg separated
¼ cup honey
Grated rind of ½ lemon
1½ cups sifted soya flour
2 teaspoons baking powder
3 tablespoons finely chopped nuts
2 tablespoons brown sugar
½ teaspoon cinnamon

Cream the butter and sugar together until fluffy. Beat in the egg yolk and half the white. Add the honey and the lemon rind. Mix thoroughly.

Sift the flour with the baking powder and stir into mixture. Knead with as little flour as possible to blend thoroughly. Roll out thin on a floured board. Spread over the surface the other half of the egg white, beaten.

Combine nuts, 2 tablespoons brown sugar and cinnamon, and sprinkle evenly over the rolled out dough. Cut into about 40 rectangular pieces and place on floured baking sheet. Bake about 12 minutes in a preheated moderate oven (350°F.) or until the dough is cooked. Transfer to a flat brown paper (or paper towels) to cool, then store in a tightly covered container.

9 Honey Nutmeg Cookies

4 cups cake flour (sifted)
¼ teaspoon nutmeg
¾ cup butter or margarine
2 teaspoons baking powder
2 cups honey
2 eggs beaten
1 lemon, grated
¼ cup milk
1½ teaspoons vanilla

Mix and sift three cups of flour with the nutmeg. Cream shortening with wooden spoon. Gradually beat in the honey. Then add eggs and grated lemon. Stir in remaining one cup of flour alternately with the milk. The dough should be stiff enough to roll.

Chill dough thoroughly in the refrigerator.

Roll out on lightly-floured board, about ½ inch thick. Cut with cookie cutter. Place on greased baking sheet and bake at 350°F. for about 12 minutes. This recipe makes about four dozen cookies.

(This is a Pennsylvania Dutch recipe.)

agyw 7/1971

fed II
L clyt 8 —
greetings. 131 to 135

8

HONEY PIES AND DESSERTS

Honey pies and desserts provide healthy, delicious eating. They have an exotic quality, elusive and provocative. Textures of pie fillings and puddings are satiny and rich.

The recipes were chosen for their interest value and ease in preparation.

Honey Cheese Pie

Pastry for 1 unbaked 9-inch pie shell
    or graham cracker crust
8 ounce package of cream cheese
    (room temperature)
3 eggs
½ cup honey

½ cup light cream (half and half may
 be used)
½ cup milk
¼ teaspoon salt
1 teaspoon grated lemon rind
1 tablespoon lemon juice

Bake pie shell 10 minutes at 425°F. Cream the
cheese. Combine beaten eggs, honey, cream, milk,
salt and lemon rind. Add egg mixture to cheese
gradually and beat until smooth. Add lemon juice.
(The mixture will be quite liquid. The cheese,
eggs, honey, cream, milk, salt and lemon rind and
juice may all be placed in a food blender and
mixed at slow speed.)

Pour mixture into partly baked pie shell. Bake in
preheated 350°F. oven for 35-40 minutes, or until
filling is firm. Chill.

May be served with topping of glazed blueber-
ries, cherries, or simply sprinkled with cinnamon.

Lemon-Honey Chiffon Pie

1 tablespoon unflavored gelatin
¼ cup cold water
4 eggs, separated
⅔ cup honey
½ teaspoon salt
½ cup lemon juice
1 teaspoon grated lemon rind
9-inch pie shell
1 cup heavy cream, if desired

Soften gelatin in cold water; set aside. Beat egg
yolks and combine with honey, salt, and lemon

juice and rind. Cook mixture over hot water until thick, stirring constantly. Add gelatin and stir to dissolve. Remove from the heat and cool.

Beat egg whites until stiff, then fold into the custard mixture. Turn into a 9-inch baked pastry shell. Chill until firm. Top with whipped cream before serving, if desired.

NOTE: This pie may be made with a graham-cracker pie shell.

Honey Apple Crisp

> *2 cups pared and sliced apples*
> *¼ cup honey*
> *1½ teaspoons lemon juice*
> *½ to ¾ cup of crumbled graham crackers*
>   *or whole wheat bread crumbs*
> *2 tablespoons butter or margarine*

Place apples in a shallow baking dish. Drizzle honey and lemon juice over the apples. Mix the crumbled crackers or bread crumbs (or a combination of the two) with the butter or margarine. Sprinkle over the top of the apples. Bake at 375°F. for 30-40 minutes or until the apples are tender.

Serve with cream and a dash of cinnamon on top—or just as is. Makes four servings, about ½ cup each.

NOTE: If apples are tart, use less lemon juice and a speck more honey.

Honey Bread Pudding

1⅔ cups day-old bread cubes
¼ cup honey
1 tablespoon butter or margarine
⅛ teaspoon salt
2 eggs, beaten
½ teaspoon vanilla
1⅔ cups hot milk

Place the bread cubes in a small baking dish. Combine the honey, butter or margarine, salt, eggs, and vanilla. Slowly stir in the milk. Pour the mixture over the bread.

Set the baking dish in a pan of hot water and bake at 350°F. for 30-40 minutes or until pudding is set.

Makes four ⅔ cup servings.

Honey Apple Betty

2 tablespoons butter or margarine
1 cup soft breadcrumbs*
1 tablespoon lemon juice
½ teaspoon grated lemon rind
2 cups pared and sliced apples
¼ cup honey
¼ cup warm water
¼ teaspoon cinnamon
¼ teaspoon nutmeg

Melt butter or margarine and stir into bread-crumbs. Add lemon juice and rind to apples. (Omit lemon if apples are very tart.)

Mix honey and water.

Place a layer of crumbs in a greased baking dish and cover with a layer of apples. Moisten with honey mixture and sprinkle with part of the seasonings. Repeat layers, ending with breadcrumbs as the top layer.

Bake at 350°F. 30-45 minutes until crumbs are well browned. (Cover baking dish for the first 15 minutes.)

Makes four servings, about ½ cup each.

*Whole wheat breadcrumbs for more nutrition and richer taste.

— End —
of chpt 8

9

MEATS, FOWLS, VEGETABLES

Honey's sweetness and texture blend well with bland meats and poultry, add body to the natural flavor of vegetables.

Pork and chicken go particularly well with honey. The recipes here given are for pork and chicken. Honey glaze may also be used on ham.

Only one recipe is given for beets but it may be used for a variety of vegetables. Also, adding *just a speck* of honey to cooked green peas, green beans, spinach, broccoli, gives them a special honey zest! Carrots and sweet potatoes are natural cronies of honey.

Polynesian Chicken

1 1-lb. 4 oz. can sliced pineapple,
*   drained*
1 broiler-fryer, cut into quarters
¼ cup prepared mustard (Dijon mustard
*   is best)*
¼ cup honey
1 teaspoon lemon juice
1 tablespoon sesame seeds

Arrange pineapple slices in a shallow baking dish. Place chicken skin-side down on pineapple.

Combine mustard, honey, lemon juice and sesame seeds. Brush over chicken, using only half the mixture. Bake uncovered at 375°F. for 30 minutes, or until brown. Turn the chicken, skin-side up. Baste with remaining sauce. Continue baking another 30 minutes, or until tender. Chicken should be puffy, and moist inside. Don't overbake.

Makes four servings. This may be served with rice pilaf and buttered fresh green peas.

Glazed Baked Chicken

2 fryer-boiler chickens, cut up (about
*   1½ pounds each)*
¾ cup fresh orange juice
2 tablespoons fresh lemon juice
¼ cup salad oil
¼ cup honey
1 teaspoon salt

½ teaspoon pepper
1 teaspoon dry mustard or curry
    powder
½ teaspoon paprika

Place the chicken pieces, skin-side down, in a
large shallow bowl or pan. Combine and blend the
rest of the ingredients to make the glazing sauce.
Pour the sauce over the chicken and rotate the
pieces until the chicken is coated completely with
sauce. Cover bowl or pan and allow to marinate in
refrigerator for several hours or overnight.

When ready to cook, remove the pieces of
chicken from the sauce and place them, skin-side
down, on a rack in a shallow pan. (Line the pan
with tinfoil to catch drippings.) Baste chicken with
sauce.

Bake at 400°F. (hot) for 30 minutes. Turn
chicken and baste with remaining sauce. Bake for
30 minutes more or until done. If chicken browns
too fast cover with foil.

Makes six to eight servings.

Exotic Pork Chops

This recipe has a Philippine heritage.

Brown four loin pork chops (¾ inch thick) in a
heavy skillet. Transfer the chops to a shallow baking dish after first seasoning with salt and pepper.

Over the chops spread a layer of partially
cooked dried apricots. (About a 6-ounce package
of apricots will do.) Cover and bake in a slow oven
(300°F.) for 30 minutes.

Remove from the oven, uncover and drizzle ½

cup honey over the top. Cover, return to oven and
bake another 15 minutes or until done.

Makes four servings.

(The same recipe may be made using fresh apple slices or fresh pinapple.)

Sweet and Sour Pork

1½ pounds pork sirloin or pork shoulder
*½ cup pancake mix (plus ½ teaspoon
  salt, ¼ teaspoon pepper and ¾ teaspoon paprika)*
½ cup milk
½ cup cooking oil
2 tablespoons butter (or margarine)

Sauce:

1 cup vinegar
1 cup pineapple juice
1 cup honey
4 tablespoons cornstarch
2 tablespoons soy sauce
2 tablespoons water
2 teaspoons salt
½ teaspoon pepper
1 13-ounce can pineapple chunks
1 green pepper
1 small sweet onion
*2 tomatoes—peeled, sliced and cut in
  wedges.*

Cut pork into bite-size pieces. Prepare batter
with pancake mix, milk, salt, pepper and paprika.
Heat oil and butter in electric skillet at 380°F. Dip

pork in batter and fry in hot oil. When browned, remove pork and hold until sauce is cooked. Drain oil from skillet.

Sauce:

In skillet, combine first 8 ingredients. Cook until clear and thickened. Add pineapple chunks, pepper, onion, and pork. Cook 3 to 4 minutes. Add tomatoes just before serving.

Serve on bed of noodles or fluffy white rice.

Honey-Glazed Beets

1 can diced or sliced beets, drained
2 tablespoons butter
3 tablespoons lemon juice
1 teaspoon grated lemon rind
½ cup honey
½ teaspoon salt
½ teaspoon pepper

Season beets with salt and pepper, lemon rind and juice. Place in casserole; cover with honey and dots of butter. Bake for about fifteen to twenty minutes at 350°F. or until glaze is just slightly brown.

(The casserole should be covered.)

The same recipe may be followed using orange juice instead of lemon juice, and carrots instead of beets. The carrots should be pre-cooked. Cooked squash may be used—hubbard, banana, acorn—whatever is available in the markets.

End y
chpt 9.

10

HONEY HAPPENINGS

Many recipes are born because of unexpected circumstances or happenings. Some come into existence because of certain taste idiosyncracies, others because of inherent frugality. The author spent one summer camping throughout Italy, France and Greece, and shared many home-cooked outdoor concoctions. What amazed her most was the marvelous dishes hatched out of stale and left-over bread, by *signorinas* and *mesdames* with large broods to feed! Necessity and availability seem to combine to inspire original food creations.

Sometimes an unexpected luncheon guest or two demands extraordinary brain cudgelling in a budget-conscious creative cuisine.

From all this recipes "happen."

Orange Ecrase

Orange ecrase has French roots—hence the term *ecrase* which means "crushed" or "smashed."

The young French housewife who gave the recipe to the author said she "adored" fresh orange juice, but she "deplored" wasting the pulp of the orange. Here's the result:

For two or three servings: Peel two or three oranges (depending on size), cut up and place in osterizer or moulinette. Let it run long enough to "smash" all the orange pulp. Drizzle in a bit of honey.

This may be served anytime—breakfast, lunch, for snacks. As a special dessert it may be served in sherbets with a glob of whipped cream or ice cream, or crushed berries.

The following happening came about as a result of an unexpected Ecuadorian guest for lunch, plus a "mistake" in mixing hamburger with honey the previous night.

Actually, the whole situation evolved around a recipe for hamburgers given to the author by a Mexican friend. The recipe called for one-half cup of honey per pound of meat. The author tried it and the result was too sweet for her taste, so she was left with about half a pound of the "honeyed hamburger mix." A package of corn tortillas in the refrigerator offered an ideal medium for absorbing some of the excess sweetness. Here's the result:

Ecuadorian Honey Tortillas

Meat mixture:
 1 pound chopped beef
 Salt and pepper to taste
 ½ cup honey

Sauté one or two chopped onions in oil. Add meat mixture. Brown gently. Add enough tomato sauce to make a spreadable mixture.

Dip each corn tortilla in hot oil. Then spread with layer of meat mixture, grated jack (or mild cheddar) cheese, and chopped black olives (if available).

Roll up tortillas and place in shallow baking dish. Cover with heavy layer of more grated cheese and pour tomato sauce over the top. Cover with tinfoil and bake in 375° oven for about twenty minutes or until cheese is melted and bubbly. Serve with a crisp chopped lettuce salad.

This should make at least a dozen tortillas. For a spicier effect, instead of using tomato sauce, you may use enchillada sauce, or a mixture of enchillada sauce with tomato purée. (Two 8-ounce cans or one 12- to 16-ounce can of tomato sauce is required.)

ONE DISH NATURAL BREAKFASTS WITH HONEY

The famous Bircher-Muesli breakfast cereal originated in Switzerland and has been adopted in many countries, including the United States. It may be purchased ready made. Here are two simple recipes for making it yourself.

Apple Bircher-Muesli No. 1
(one portion)

Soak 1 tablespoon of whole oats in 2 tablespoons of water overnight.

In the morning add the juice of ½ lemon and 1 tablespoon rich cream (or milk). Mix well.

Grate an apple (well washed but unpeeled) into the mixture. Stir well. Add honey to taste—about ½ to one teaspoon.

Apple Bircher-Muesli No. 2
(one portion)

Soak 1 tablespoon wheat germ and 1 tablespoon whole oats in 4 tablespoons of water overnight (in refrigerator).

Next morning add 1 teaspoon lemon juice, one teaspoon honey, one tablespoon cream or milk and one shredded unpeeled apple. Add chopped nuts or sunflower seeds.

Note: Both the above may be made with fresh berries, bananas, peaches—any fresh fruit in season.

SPECIAL ETHNIC HONEY DELIGHTS

Greek Loukoumades (Honey Puffs)

3 to 4 cups sifted flour
2 packages yeast
½ cup warm water
1 cup warm milk
¼ cup sugar
1 teaspoon salt
2 eggs beaten
½ cup melted butter
cooking oil
honey
cinnamon

Soften yeast in warm water. Pour the warm milk into a large bowl; add salt and sugar. Stir in the yeast and beaten eggs. Add the melted butter. Beat well.

Gradually add the sifted flour beating continuously until the batter is thick and smooth. Cover and let rise in a warm place for several hours. (The dough may be made at night and allowed to stand overnight.)

Heat three to four inches of cooking oil in a deep sauce-pan. (A french-frying pan is excellent.) Stir the batter well. Drop a tablespoonful of batter into the oil. Cook until the batter puffs and is golden brown on all sides.

Drain. Place on a platter in layers, sprinking each layer with cinnamon and warm honey diluted in a little water. Serve immediately. Makes about three dozen.

Jewish Teiglach (Sweetmeats)

4 eggs
3 tablespoons oil
4 cups flour
2 cups honey and 1 cup sugar
Ground ginger, up to 1 tablespoon
    (according to taste)
Raisins, filberts (optional)

Beat eggs. Add oil and enough flour to make a soft dough. Meanwhile mix the honey, sugar and ginger in a saucepan and allow to come to a slow boil.

Pinch off pieces of the dough mixture, about the size of a walnut. Wrap around a raisin or a piece of filbert. Form into balls and drop into the cooking honey.

Allow to cook uncovered until the dough balls rise. Cover, lower heat and continue cooking slowly for about 45 minutes, until a warm golden brown.

At this point there are two ways to serve the *teiglach.* They may be dished into a bowl with the syrup and eaten with a spoon. Or they may be lifted out individually from the syrup and rolled in chopped nuts and placed on a platter.

(*Teiglach* are a traditional sweet for the Passover holiday, when potato flour is substituted for the regular flour.)

Turkish Paste (Sweetmeat)

5 tablespoons gelatin
½ cup cold water
¼ cup hot water
1 cup honey
1 cup sugar
¼ teaspoon salt
½ cup orange juice
3 tablespoons lemon juice
Green coloring and mint flavoring
                or
Red coloring and almond flavoring
1 cup finely chopped nuts

Soften the gelatin in the cold water for 5 minutes. Bring the hot water, sugar and honey to the boiling point. Add salt and gelatin. Stir until the gelatin has dissolved. Simmer for 20 minutes.

Remove from the fire. When cool add the orange and lemon juice, coloring and flavoring. Stir again before pouring into shallow *wet* pan. The layer of paste should be about an inch thick.

Let stand in a cool place overnight. (May be placed in the refrigerator.)

Next day dip a sharp knife into boiling water, cut the candy into cubes and roll in powdered sugar.

Russian Honey Beet Jam

1 pound beets
1 cup honey
gingerroot
almonds or hazelnuts

Wash, peel and cut beets into ½ inch slices. Cook in water until tender. Drain.

Add the honey and cook until thick. Flavor with gingerroot or ground ginger to taste.

Serve cold with nuts.

California Honey Candy Rolls (Uncooked)

1 cup dry milk powder
1 cup plain or chunk-style peanut butter
1 cup honey
½ teaspoon vanilla
Additional peanuts if desired.

Mix all the ingredients together. Shape into bite-size rolls. Keep in refrigerator. They make a wonderful in-between or after school snack—a pure, healthy candy!

British Honey and Nut, Cold Cake (Unbaked)

1 pound stale whole-wheat breadcrumbs
4 ounces margarine or butter (or half and half)

— Chpt. 10 —

Juice of one lemon
½ pound honey (1 cup)
¼ pound soft brown sugar (½ cup)
2 ounces chopped nuts or dried coconut.

Melt sugar, butter and honey together in a thick saucepan and boil for two minutes. Stir in breadcrumbs, lemon juice and nuts. Beat well. Allow to cool.

Turn on to a plate or dish and shape into a round or square cake about 2 to 2½ inches thick. Place in the refrigerator. Slice and serve cold with tea.

British Honey Cakes

1 cup wheat or oat flakes
1 tablespoon honey
1 tablespoon milk

Mix all well together, form into small cakes and serve with stewed fruit. Do not bake.

— End of chpt. 10 —

11

HONEY AND ECOLOGY

Ecology is a vital subject of the day. Politicians, housewives, students, children, businessmen, are all talking ecology. Newspapers carry full-page ads almost every day about pollution. Old-fashioned polluting detergents are being replaced on market shelves by "pollution-free" detergents. Consumers are beginning to examine more carefully the labels on packages, to determine contents and ingredients before buying. There's a new thoughtfulness dawning in America about "purity" in food.

Honeybees and honey are deeply involved in ecology. If pesticides are used indiscriminately honeybees will suffer and production of honey will diminish; more serious, plants will not be pollinated and will rapidly die off. The quantity and quality of honey may be adversely affected. Already the effects of pesticides are being noticed by honeybee farmers.

At this writing public hearings are being held in many areas of the United States to consider adoption of regulations with respect to the use of pesticides. Recently such a hearing was held in Ohio, a state actively involved with honey production. Regulations were adopted providing that application of pesticides which are hazardous to honeybees must be halted when pollinating insects are actively working in the target areas.

Provisions were also made requiring that each pesticide carry a special warning on the label indicating that it is especially toxic to honeybees. Further regulations were enacted stating that any such toxic pesticide may not be dispensed over more than ½ acre in which the crop plant is in flower unless all registered apiaries located within ½ mile of the treatment site were given not less than 24 hours' advance notice.

Other states have adopted similar regulations. But despite all the regulations apiarists are deeply concerned. Certain residue of the pesticides remains in the area, and winds carry powder or liquid sprays to locations other than the treatment site.

Meanwhile the U.S. Department of Agriculture is engaged in research to determine ways to protect honeybees from pesticides, and other studies are being made to develop strains of bees with natural resistance to certain pesticides.

There is talk about restricting or possibly banning the use of certain pesticides. The controversial DDT has been banned in many states.

In California the Department of Agriculture recently introduced a mobile chemistry laboratory which travels through the farming areas of the state. Random samples of field crops are checked before harvest; and if the pesticide residue is above safety level the farmer is notified. Sometimes the crop can be saved by holding it a few days; other times it has to be plowed under. According to chemist, C. J. Miller, of the California Agriculture Department—one of the chemists who works in the mobile laboratory—most farmers are cooperative; they don't want to take a chance of being fined, let alone losing a crop.

But despite hearings, research, regulations and crop-checking, the use of pesticides continues to be an issue of great concern among ecology- and health-minded individuals. They fear the entire balance of nature is being destroyed. One experienced observer, after a tour through the grape-growing regions of the San Joaquin Valley, California, remarked that "even the birds are disappearing."

In the days before insecticides the only enemies the honeybee had to contend with were natural: nest-raiding animals, tornadoes, drought, floods, destructive insects. But the honeybee could always go elsewhere to find honey-making ingredients. Even if a plague of locusts or weevils destroyed a crop, bees would either decrease their "population" and their requirements, or find another source.

With today's modern methods of crop-dusting from the air, it's not always possible for the bees to find uncontaminated sources. Wide use of pesticides became prevalent some time after World War II with the advent of huge corporation farms. It's difficult to control plant-destroying pests on vast acreage without the use of pesticides. Small farmers could manage to control destructive insects. Some used what they call natural control, by planting certain combinations of crops—or what is referred to as "mixed culture."

"Mixed culture" farming is popular in Europe,

especially in Germany where large plots of land are being subdivided into small gardens. Much of the land is owned by associations which rent out space to its members; some is privately owned by companies or individuals, who rent out plots.

The basic concept of mixed culture farming is to combine crops which help one another. For example, it's been found that smell secretions of one plant are a good defense against insects which attack a neighboring plant. Between short-leafed early carrots and leeks there is such a mutual relationship. The enemy of the carrot is the carrot fly; the enemies of the leek are the onion fly and the leek moth. The smell of the leek is distasteful to the carrot fly, so it ignores the carrots. Likewise, the smell of the carrots is distasteful to the onion fly and leek moth—so it avoids the leeks!

Marigolds give off an acrid smell that repels certain aphids. Certain root secretions of plants affect insects and other plants. Experiments are constantly being made to determine "companion" plants. The whole idea is copied from nature, where in a field left to grow wild and free a conglomeration of plants grow harmoniously without blight.

This type of "controlled" farming is developing popularity among many health-minded people in the United States, especially in Southern California where some fruits or vegetables may be grown all year round.

All through Europe—France, Germany, England, Italy, and other countries—people utilize every square inch of soil. Whenever possible each family has at least a salad garden. During World War II city people in the United States farmed their victory gardens, usually located in neighborhood empty lots. But today empty lots are fast disappearing.

The surge of interest in home gardening is viewed by some sociologists as part of a desire to get back to nature. It ties in with the new interest in health foods and honey. Almost every supermarket has a health food section where a shopper may find whole grain cereals, unbleached flour, many varieties of honey, wheat germ, carob powder, soya flour, sunflower seeds, pumpkin seeds and many other health foods.

The term "ecology" is broadening—reaching into homes, into city councils. Politicians pay attention to outcries from citizens against the use of insecticides in public parks and along public avenues.

Not long ago in Arcadia, a small town on the outskirts of Los Angeles, hordes of aphids threatened to destroy beautiful silver maple trees which line the streets. In former years the town fathers called in an insecticide sprayer. Today, in 1971, they called in an entomologist who recommended a course of treatment to rid the trees of aphids by importing larvae from the green lacewing fly.

Workers made paper streamers from brown grocery bags, covered the streamers with the larvae and hung the streamers on the trees. The larvae are expected to migrate to the tree branches and leaves. When they hatch thousands of green lacewing flies will feed on the aphids. Meanwhile the flies will lay more larvae, and on and on the cycle will go.

A similar incident occurred in the town of Claremont, also on the outskirts of Los Angeles, where instead of using insecticides to rid the town's trees of aphids, the city authorities purchased thousands of ladybugs and let them loose among the trees.

Ladybugs and green lacewing flies seem to thrive on aphids!

In the battle for the environment the survival of the honeybee and her sources for honey loom greater as each succeeding year finds the absorption of more "green" space. In California alone, fields which were once covered with grapevines, orange, grapefruit and lemon trees, and wild flowers, now are covered with concrete and tract homes. Subdividers say "people must have a place to live." Ecologists say "people must have a *healthy* place to live."

If the present interest and zeal to save the environment continues and more people join the ranks of those who are committed to reclaim a healthy world for themselves and their children, the honeybee will continue to thrive and make honey. And man will continue to work better, play better, live better and love better because of it!

_ The End -

AVON ◆ NEW LEADER IN GOURMET COOKERY

160

THE BIG BESTSELLERS
ARE AVON BOOKS!

Facing the Lions Tom Wicker	19307	$1.75
High Empire Clyde M. Brundy	18994	$1.75
The Kingdom L. W. Henderson	18978	$1.75
To Die in California Newton Thornburg	18622	$1.50
The Last of the Southern Girls Willie Morris	18614	$1.50
The Hungarian Game Roy Hayes	18986	$1.75
The Wolf and the Dove Kathleen E. Woodiwiss	18457	$1.75
The Priest Ralph McInerny	18192	$1.75
Sweet Savage Love Rosemary Rogers	17988	$1.75
How I Found Freedom In An Unfree World Harry Browne	17772	$1.95
I'm OK—You're OK Thomas A. Harris, M.D.	14662	$1.95
Jonathan Livingston Seagull Richard Bach	14316	$1.50
Open Marriage George and Nena O'Neill	14084	$1.95

Where better paperbacks are sold, or directly from the publisher. Include 15¢ per copy for mailing; allow three weeks for delivery.

Avon Books, Mail Order Dept., 250 West 55th Street, New York, N.Y. 10019